Praise for
LET ME OUT

"Fear is one of life's biggest roadblocks, which is why Peter Himmelman's book is so important. *Let Me Out* gets to the heart of how we can keep fear from limiting our potential by tapping into our inner resilience, creativity, and strength. There's deep wisdom here along with very practical tools for translating our ideas into the real world."

—Arianna Huffington, cofounder and editor in chief
of the *Huffington Post*

"Peter Himmelman's brainchild, *Let Me Out,* is a scientifically solid, humanly inspiring, personally transformative approach to liberating innovative ideas and inspiring creative action. Himmelman's humanity and humor make the journey both a pleasure and whole lot of fun!"

—Daniel J. Siegel, MD,
clinical professor of psychiatry, David Geffen School of Medicine at UCLA;
executive director, Mindsight Institute; and author of *Mindsight,*
The Developing Mind, and *New York Times* bestseller *Brainstorm*

"*Let Me Out* taught me that finding my voice was as courageous as learning how to walk."

—Eric Roth, Oscar-winning screenwriter
(*Forrest Gump, The Curious Case of Benjamin Button*)

"Peter Himmelman is an award-winning musician, and he knows what it takes to overcome fear and unlock our creative potential. In *Let Me Out,* his energy, humanity, and imagination literally leap off the page. I can't wait to share it with my readers and my students."

—Adam Grant, Wharton School professor and author of
New York Times bestsellers *Originals* and *Give and Take*

LET ME OUT

LET ME OUT

Unlock Your Creative Mind
and Bring Your Ideas to Life

Peter Himmelman

A TarcherPerigee Book

tarcherperigee

An imprint of Penguin Random House LLC
375 Hudson Street
New York, New York 10014

Most TarcherPerigee books are available at special quantity discounts for bulk purchase for sales promotions, premiums, fund-raising, and educational needs. Special books or book excerpts also can be created to fit specific needs. For details, write:
SpecialMarkets@penguinrandomhouse.com.

LIBRARY OF CONGRESS CATALOGING-IN-PUBLICATION DATA
Names: Himmelman, Peter, author.
Title: Let me out : unlock your creative mind and bring your ideas to life /
Peter Himmelman.
Description: New York : TarcherPerigee, 2016.
Identifiers: LCCN 2016026855 (print) | LCCN 2016036720 (ebook) | ISBN
9780143110958 (hardback) | ISBN 9781101992722
Subjects: LCSH: Creative ability. | Creative ability in business. |
Self-realization. | BISAC: BUSINESS & ECONOMICS / Motivational. | BUSINESS
& ECONOMICS / Skills.
Classification: LCC BF408 .H496 2016 (print) | LCC BF408 (ebook) | DDC
153.3/5—dc23
LC record available at https://lccn.loc.gov/2016026855

Printed in the United States of America
1   3   5   7   9   10   8   6   4   2

Book design by Patrice Sheridan

Dedicated to my father, David, a kind and fearless man

who instilled in me the notion that it is perfectly natural

to take the fruits of my imagination and make them real

CONTENTS

INTRODUCTION

ARE YOU AFRAID of your dreams?

I'm not talking about your nightmares. I mean the good ones—your hopes, your blue-sky aspirations. I know it sounds a little odd to be frightened of your own better future, but think about it. . . . There's an internal critic in our heads that's always terrified, always on the lookout for danger. I'm not saying it isn't helpful or even a lifesaver at times. If you were going to do something truly stupid, it'd be the first to shout: "Hey, idiot, don't stick your head in that bonfire!" But that same critic can hold you back. Wanting to be an opera singer or an anesthesiologist or wanting to run a marathon, or lose twenty pounds, or pilot a bathyscaphe or tell your mother you love her . . . these aren't fires to be avoided—they're flames you want to fan. So why does this protective voice regularly perceive these good dreams as threats and prevent you from pursuing them? Why is it that you're so much better at putting the brakes on your creative ideas than you are at making them come true? And what if you could change that?

In the fall of 2011, artist Candy Chang found an abandoned building in New Orleans and turned it into a touchstone of hope, in part by using hearse-black paint and the word *die*. It's hard to picture anything that grim eliciting optimism, but Chang's idea was as profound as it was elegant. After painting the entire building black, she stenciled this declaration on its side countless times, in white:

Since she did this, hundreds of people have visited the site to fill in their own answers with colored chalk.

Her experiment has since been covered extensively in media and replicated in cities all over the world.

So before we embark, think for a moment about the "abandoned buildings" in your life—the goals you've given up on, or put on hold for so long you no longer recognize them. How would you fill in that sentence? "Before I die, I want to_____."

I TOO HAVE experienced firsthand what it's like to feel the pain and the joy of pursuing a dream. I'm a musician, a songwriter, and a performer. I've made twenty critically acclaimed recordings, including five albums of children's music. I've had three major-label recording contracts. I've toured the United States at least thirty times. I've even performed in Soviet Central Asia (to my knowledge I'm the only American rock musician to have ever played the Lenin Palace of Culture and Sport, in Tajikistan). I've composed music for several films and network television shows, and I've been nominated for an Emmy and a Grammy. Ever since the fifth grade I dreamed of being a rock star, and after years of hard work and abundant good fortune, I actually became one.

Unfortunately, in the past few years the Internet has caused major disruptions in my business. In case you haven't heard: Almost nobody's paying for music anymore. My cousin Lawrence, a diamond dealer from Chicago, asked me to explain the problem. By way of metaphor, I told him to cup his hands under his computer screen and imagine that all the diamonds he is trying so hard to sell simply fall into his hands for free. "That's rough," was all he had to say. Indeed. As a result of the changes, I had to answer the question of what I wanted to do with my life—again.

The radical shifts I had to undergo led me to a place where you might be this very moment, where being creative and following your dreams isn't just some fun idea; it's imperative. No matter if you're a high school student, a housewife, a parasailing instructor, or the CEO of an organic kale distributorship, you will find out sooner or later that the way you've been doing things up until now will eventually need to change. In my case, the way I used to do things definitely didn't work any longer. The upheavals I was experiencing prompted a serious need to re-create and rebrand myself. I was forced to conjure up the same red-hot creative resources I had brandished as a young man. I never considered that what I'd been doing when I was twenty-two, and what I'd spent my adult life learning to master, would simply stop being effective financially when I hit fifty-two.

That's when I understood: It wasn't a lack of knowing what I wanted to do that was holding me back. It was listening to that overprotective voice I mentioned earlier—my inner critic. Listening to that negative voice is something I've always been expert at, and hearing it kvetch that my dreams were no longer possible, that I should be confused about where to turn next, was (at the time anyway) absolutely mesmerizing. I eventually realized that I just needed to find a new way of doing what I'd loved all along: writing music, performing, and working with other people to create music. Even though all the negative internal chatter was leaving me pretty depressed, I still believed I had something of value to share that the Internet could never take away. It was around this time that I had what in retrospect seems like a lightning bolt of inspiration:

This thing I've been doing most of my life—songwriting, with its unique combination of strict structure and free-associative poetics—is actually a perfect metaphor for teaching about how ideas go from the mind and into the world! My next move was clear: *Using music and the same techniques I use to write songs, I would start a business that helps individuals and organizations become more creative and fulfilled.*

So what happened next? Not a damn thing. For almost two years I just sat on the idea like a duck on an egg. How, you ask, could I not follow through on such a critical insight into my future? Well, endlessly contemplating going on safari in Botswana is great, but until you actually pack your bags and hop on a plane, you can dream about the Duba concession in the far north of the Okavango all you want and wind up still at your desk . . . still on the sofa . . . still lying awake in bed at three in the morning wondering, "Why am I still here?" If you've ever had this experience of stalling and never quite getting down to the business of finishing anything, you're certainly not alone.

Why was it so difficult for me to get a cup of coffee, turn on my computer, and start outlining the broad strokes of my new company? Why didn't I start going through my address book to single out contacts I thought could help? Why didn't I follow through with more concrete ideas and repeat the same process for several months until I'd achieved something tangible?

For starters, I spent too little time thinking about how the new business might look in success and too much time worrying about how I might feel when it inevitably failed to get off the ground. I spent time worrying about why it was all too hard, why I was underqualified to speak in front of large groups of people, and about the many ways I could embarrass myself for even trying. I'd answer e-mails, I'd talk on the phone, I'd browse the Internet— "Hey, I wonder what it costs to take a scuba diving vacation in Bali." Every imaginable distraction called me away from the task of actually sitting down and mapping out the first steps of my idea.

And then one day, I don't know exactly how to describe it . . . I simply stopped the mulling and started the doing.

It was July 14, 2011, to be exact. Why? Why that specific date? What happened that morning that distinguished it from all my other false starts? What unusual impetus propelled me that day from dreaming to sitting my ass in a chair and beginning the actual work? Somehow, I'd crossed an invisible line. There was an internal wince. The inner critic roared with disapproval—and then, the intangible became tangible for the first time.

I acted differently that day and did three simple things. First, I set a timer and gave myself fifteen minutes to create a list of potential names for my company, then I gave myself ten minutes to make some thumbnail sketches of logo ideas, and finally, I took ten minutes to look into purchasing domain names. That was it. These were three remarkably easy tasks, three tiny ideas. But the radical difference between that fateful morning and so many others was that I stopped the *negative thinking* and started taking the small but definitive *actions* toward my goal. They were not earth-shattering accomplishments, to be sure, but they were actions nonetheless.

The concepts I continued to research from that day on became the basis for processes that underpin this entire book, processes by which anyone can learn how to make their ideas come to life. There are small leaps of faith I'll ask you to take as we go down this path, but for the most part, I am going to show you a clear, practical route for success. Freeing yourself from the constraints of your fear is how you will reveal your innate creativity. I will show you a system that can be learned, practiced, and repeated. The techniques I will teach you in this book have been proven to work, and the more you learn to trust yourself, the easier your own transformational leap will become.

INTRODUCING BIG MUSE

My company, which I eventually called Big Muse, officially launched August 10, 2011. That's the date I gave my first seminar, at an artists studio near the Santa Monica airport—walked out into the spotlight and showed a group of skeptical but curious strangers who'd never before tried writing a song the process by which they could overcome the fear of trying something completely new. They silenced their doubts and moved step-by-step from simply being able to articulate their dreams to a state of transformational possibility: a tangible, physical result—a finished song. The song became their symbol, their metaphor—their proof that the process works. My finished song was Big Muse itself. Your finished song is *your* dream. And by learning to break your dream into small pieces, working on those small pieces without delay, and constantly course-correcting when necessary to ensure that you are pursuing something connected with your truest values and desires, you can achieve almost anything. In this book, as in my seminars, I will show you how to do the following:

1. Create more fearlessly
2. Communicate more potently
3. Finish projects that have stayed in the "bits and pieces" phase forever
4. Make your ideas take shape in the real world

In less than two years I went from merely dreaming about a new way to channel my music to working with Banana Republic, the Gap, Adobe, McDonald's, Frito-Lay, Kellogg School of Management at Northwestern University, the Wharton School at the University of Pennsylvania, and many others. I was helping individuals within each organization learn to channel their own Big Muse, silence their inner critic, and accomplish real goals.

Big Muse works and is so unique because of something I call the Bilateral Brain Bottle Opener Theory, or BLBBOT. Actually, no, I don't call it that; I just made it up—but opening your brain is pretty much what happens when you apply ideas. Big Muse combines scientifically proven cognitive methods with my own artistic methods to convert and unite left- *and* right-brained thinking into action. In this way I'm utilizing some of the techniques of American psychiatrist Aaron T. Beck, who developed the science of cognitive therapy back in the 1960s.

The theory in a nutshell is that someone like me, for example, who strongly believes that reinventing himself and starting a new career in his fifties is unrealistic, will be led by those beliefs to avoid taking the necessary action steps to accomplish his goal. Not taking action will further support those negative assumptions in a sort of cyclical fashion until the Great Wall of Pessimism is erected. When you take what's known as "adaptive steps" (those small parts of a goal that help a person to see only the small stones that make up the wall and not the imposing wall itself), negative beliefs can be exchanged for other more desirable beliefs, taking your dream out of your head and into the real world.

But these are just concepts. What defines Big Muse and makes it so different from virtually every other self-help philosophy you may have tried are the techniques I'm about to share with you, techniques derived from applied artistic experience. In reading this book you will learn how to take abstract intellectual models and translate them into real tools for creative practice through connective storytelling, stirring metaphors, and powerful and deceptively simple Brain Bottle Opener exercises, each of which comes with annotations on its real-world applications.

I've seen the Big Muse method work in real time, unblocking the minds of thousands of different people with completely different dreams:

- A high school senior in Minneapolis who dreamed of becoming a professional photographer. She followed the principles in this book and in six months sold more than two thousand dollars' worth of photos at her first gallery showing.

- An IT executive in San Antonio who initially dreamed of writing just one song. He followed the principles in this book and in less than a year recorded and released his first full-length CD—and it's currently getting airplay on a Texas radio station.

- A marketing director for an international restaurant chain who dreamed of stopping his drug and alcohol problem. He followed the principles in this book and got himself into a 12-step program. He's been sober one full year at the time of this writing. (He also earned the respect of his bosses and got a promotion.)

- A wounded warrior from Virginia who dreamed of saving a marriage that was on the verge of divorce. He followed the principles outlined in these pages, and has become a more expressive, more demonstrative husband. His family life is finding its way back on track.

In every case these people achieved their goals by making that leap of faith and then taking that first step.

Our time on earth is limited and there are important things we all want to accomplish before we run out of it. The journey we undertake together in these pages leads to a treasure—one you may have buried in your heart long ago—and reading this book will help you find it.

I'm not going to show you how to merely mull over your dreams or contemplate them endlessly . . . or ruminate or ponder or dwell or obsess. I'm going to help you to pluck your dreams from your head and plant them here in time and space. Whether you're a social studies teacher who wants to fly a plane, an actuary who wants to play the jazz trombone, a Navy SEAL who wants to write poetry, a special education counselor who wants to make artisan cheeses, a COO of a huge corporation who wants to spend more time with your family, a tenth-grader who wants to learn to play the ukulele, a bicycle mechanic who wants to be a Buddhist monk, or a Buddhist monk who wants to be a bicycle mechanic, you've already taken the first step by reading this far. Give yourself credit and consider it the first step on the trek of a lifetime.

THINK ABOUT THAT blank space again: Before I die, I want to _____, that dream you've held so close to the vest that perhaps you're the only one who knows about it. If my story of stalling, always stalling, and never actually getting anything accomplished sounds familiar, read on. This book will pinpoint the internal forces that keep you from getting down to business, and it will show you how to outsmart them. Take a break from your doubts and fears, and get ready to let out your own Big Muse.

PART ONE

THE CHALLENGES

Don't ask what the world needs. Ask what makes you come alive and go do that. Because what the world needs is people who have come alive.

-Howard Thurman

CHAPTER 1

MEET MARV

EXPLAINING THE NEGATIVE VOICE WITHIN

Why do so many of our best ideas go down the drain with the soap before we can even reach for the towel? It's not that way for everyone, is it? We all know people who are able to follow through on their ideas and we wonder: Are they born with certain gifts the rest of us lack? Do they share some common set of actions or beliefs?

I always hear people say that if you want it, "just do it"—as if just doing it were the most natural thing in the universe: Just lose weight, just start a business, just find a wife, just learn to draw, just learn to fly a helicopter.

Why is just doing it so hard? It's hard because we've got a voice in our heads that's constantly yammering about our deficiencies and filling us with fear. But what exactly is that annoying, negative voice? What is its function? It must have an important one, because everyone I've ever met has got the same voice inside. My firm belief, and I'll illustrate this idea extensively throughout the book, is that this negative voice does not represent an enemy, as some writers have suggested. Rather, it's a very real and integral part of our psychological makeup, one that cares strongly about our own survival. In that sense, it's not something to be eradicated or pushed away (as if we *could* push it away). It's a part of us that needs to be valued and understood. It's funny how the needs of this internal critic are so similar to our own needs. The similarity exists because "it" is us.

To humanize this internal critic, I've given it a name: Marv. Marv is what my wife and I would call our oldest son, Isaac, whenever we traveled and he'd start complaining, or asking ridiculous questions of the "Are we there yet?" variety. We'd ask, "Who let Marv in the car?" By the way, if your name is Marv, take no umbrage. I mean no offense. Please just think of MARV as an acronym for: **M**ajorly **A**fraid of **R**evealing **V**ulnerability.

THE KEYS TO THE CAR: SPECIFIC, PRESENT, AND TRUE

Just as my wife and I wouldn't have dreamed of letting our little Marv behind the wheel, we shouldn't entertain the thought of letting Internal Critic Marv take our dreams on a wrong-way drive. Yet how often do our boldest plans wind up in a ditch or stalled on the side of the road? What we need is a map—one that shows not just a destination, but directions on how to get there. We also need to keep Marv in the backseat, buckled up in a safety belt where he belongs. Marv will give you space and allow your dreams to manifest themselves if you keep the following three qualities in mind. Your dreams must be:

> **Specific:** Dream as big as you like, but make sure your dream is specified and broken down into small, actionable pieces. Don't think, "I want to become a baseball star" without also thinking, "I'm going to the ballpark now to practice my swing for thirty minutes."
>
> **Present:** Don't just think, "I'll start practicing sometime midweek." Instead, think, "I'll go to the ballpark at 10:35 this morning"—and then actually go.
>
> **True:** Don't pursue the dream of being a baseball star because your dad pressured you into it. The dream itself must be self-generated and it must be something you want to pursue, for your own sake and of your own volition.

It's a point of pride for many of us when we consider the dozens of times in our lives when our ideas were undervalued or criticized but we went forward with them anyway. Our sense of pride wasn't necessarily for the things we'd eventually created, but for the very fact that we overcame Marv's voice and the critical voices of others. Unchecked external criticism, such as bad reviews or people not buying tickets to your show, always generates internal criticism. And people's negative comments aren't mere gasoline for Marv; they're rocket fuel. He becomes hyper-energized and goads you into quitting whenever he hears others criticize you. Why is this?

You see, Marv fears for our safety and well-being. As infants, when we depended on our parents for our very survival, Marv was there as well, and he sensed correctly that if we were abandoned we would die. Apparently he still hasn't gotten over that frightening realization, because though we've all grown up in the physical sense, most of us have never fully outgrown those primal concerns surrounding abandonment and our own mortality.

The fear that we feel when we try something new, something particularly challenging, isn't some petty worry; it's actually a mortal fear. That's why when we want to reinvent ourselves by following our dreams, Marv's sway over us is still so strong. But like I mentioned earlier, Marv isn't trying to hurt us; he's trying to save our skins. If a voracious lion were on the attack, it would be Marv who compelled us to flee for our lives. He's ever vigilant, with his hand constantly on the lever that squirts the adrenaline into our bloodstreams and the lifesaving anxiety into our brains. He's got such a one-track mind about helping us that he simply hasn't heard the news: Marv, our lives are not in danger anymore, so please relax!

WHY MARV CAN'T RELAX: WOOLLY MAMMOTHS AND THE BRAIN SCIENCE OF THE INNER CRITIC

Nobel Prize–winning neurobiologist Roger Sperry suggested that human beings are essentially of two minds. His pioneering brain-hemisphere research in the early 1960s led to a well-known (and largely misunderstood) theory about left- and right-brained thinking. The idea is that the left brain is oriented toward straightforward, analytical, numerical, this-is-the-way-things-are type thinking; while the right brain is oriented toward a dreamy, this-is-the-way-things-could-be type of thinking. While many leading psychologists still support Sperry's idea, those in the field of neuroscience have never fully accepted it, believing instead that the brain is far more complicated than his dual-hemisphere theory suggests.

But regardless of where creativity is located in the brain, human beings clearly have two distinct capacities: one for logical thinking and one for more fluid, amorphous thinking. So for example, when you get up to brush your teeth in the morning, your left brain's logical functions will have all the warmth of an engrossed police detective: *Just the facts, ma'am. Grab toothbrush. Put toothpaste on toothbrush. Put toothbrush in mouth. Scrub.* The logical mind is geared toward survival as well. It's ever on the alert in case a woolly mammoth or some other beast from our primordial past attacks us. The logical mind's no-nonsense orientation comes in handy when we need to get out the door and on our way to an important appointment.

The more fluid right brain functions, by contrast, are creative and deal well with constantly shifting dynamics. The fluid brain favors artistic considerations. It is oriented to the metaphorical, considers all possibilities, and thrives on weighing endless variations. It also loves the realm of dreams and desires. So let's pretend for a minute that you could shut off your analytical mind, leaving only your fluid mind to brush your teeth. It might sound something like this:

> Oh my god! The toothbrush handle . . . it's pink. And translucent! And when I hold it up to the light, it's like a neon eel. Wait a minute—what is color anyway? And how did cavemen clean their teeth? T-t-t-teeth . . . I love the hard sound of the letter T. . . .

No doubt, you'd have a lot of fun, but you'd never get your mouth clean and you'd miss that crucial appointment.

But how does this all relate to Marv? Simple. There is a crucial part in the creative process in which you have to let the fluid part of the mind dominate. You can't think about reviews, impressing friends, your paycheck, or the size of your trophy. Not that those are irrelevant concerns, but they exist strictly on the analytical mind's home turf, with things like judgments, measurements, and return on investment.

When you embark on making dreams specific, present, and true, you have to start by diving in and immersing yourself in the work at hand. You have to surrender control. The brain's more fluid capacities are built to brave the unknown and all its possibilities. The analytical part of the brain, still on the lookout for a woolly mammoth after all these eons, doesn't like that. And so, to shake you out of the dream state that's about to commence—that is, being immersed in the warm flow of a project, where you'll lose track of time and drop your guard—it's going to play dirty.

Here's what the analytical mind and its pal, the meek and methodical Mr. Marv, might say to you. See how many of these inner-critic potshots sound familiar as you think about getting something accomplished:

"This idea is really stupid."
"You know all your friends will laugh at this."
"What makes you think you have anything to say?"
"What's in the fridge?"
"Isn't it time to check your e-mail again?"
"This lighting isn't quite right, is it?"

Marv is going to bombard you with distracting thoughts. When it's told it's not in control anymore, the analytical brain fights for your survival. Why? Because you can't afford to shift gears when there's an enraged woolly mammoth just around the corner.

Now this can come in handy—you wouldn't want to daydream about writing a children's book while you're walking down a menacing city street at night. But in the overwhelming majority of situations, the challenge remains one of (a) calling off Marv's mammoth patrol, and (b) increasing the chances for what I call an HourGlass moment—that sacred time when an idea is birthed through action, with the fluid part of the brain leading the way.

But as you know from personal experience, Marv isn't going to give up easily. And of all the weapons at his disposal, perhaps none is more potent than those remembered critical voices we met in the throes of our youthful uncertainty.

MARV AND CRITICISM: THE UNUSUAL CASE OF MR. FUFF AND THE FLYING SONIC FOOTBALL

I know certain people who insist they're impervious to criticism and Marv's warnings. For your own good, don't believe them. They're just plain lying. The image of these people skipping through life untouched by anything but their own invariably positive muse does not correlate with reality. Everyone hates rejection. And the problem isn't so much that these folks are lying—which they are— it's that we believe such people exist, and then we feel horrible we're not like them, that we're somehow deficient.

Let me assure you again, everybody is affected by criticism. We love it when people praise our work and we abhor it when they dismiss it. That's human nature, and it's unchanging. The only difference is that some of us are stopped in our tracks by the critical voices, while others of us keep going. On my path to becoming a professional musician, I've experienced countless disparaging moments. Here's one:

It was 1980. I was twenty years old, living in Minneapolis and a revolutionary new dance song called "Funkytown" by Lipps Inc. ruled the charts. The damn thing was everywhere: on the radio, in elevators, at clubs, even playing overhead in the frozen-food section at the Red Owl. As fate would have it, "Funkytown" was written by Steven Greenberg, the multitalented drummer of the Kinship, Minneapolis's most popular bar mitzvah and wedding band. Soon, I was going to his place once or twice a week to play him demos of things I'd written, to get his opinion, and to interest him in helping me with my career. Truth be told, there wasn't a lot of pleasure in taking my stuff to him for an evaluation. After all, it was so easy for Steve to criticize my music. All he needed to do was raise his eyebrow or give a little laugh, as if what he was hearing was the stupidest idea ever. Steve was a gatekeeper, or so I thought, and all my energies at the time were spent trying to create something I thought he'd like.

One afternoon I sat in my bedroom and wrote a song I was extremely pleased with. It was about a friend of my parents named Erwin Fuff. Mr. Fuff was odd. He'd been a Holocaust survivor, and I'd heard stories of him running alone through the woods in Poland as a young child. A few days before I wrote the song, my mom called me into her room and told me the police had found Mr. Fuff's wife, Riva, lying dead in their kitchen. Mr. Fuff had killed her. Since he'd had a history of mental illness, the prosecutor felt there was no need for a trial. Erwin Fuff went straight to a mental institution, where they pumped him full of so much Thorazine (an antipsychotic drug) that he was only semiconscious most of the time. The trouble was that in the early mornings, the brief time between when the previous day's dose wore off and the new day's dose was given, Mr. Fuff would regain some degree of consciousness and could feel some of the horrible grief and shame over having murdered his wife. It was during such a small window of lucidity that he took his own life, just days after arriving at the hospital.

The song I wrote was called "Cursed with What It Means." The chorus went like this:

She will sleep forever—you'll be high on Thorazine
She will sleep forever—you are cursed with what it means

I raced to Steve Greenberg's place, cassette in hand. This was a whole new style of music, dark and spare with intense lyrics based on a true story, and I knew he was going to love it. I put the cassette in his giant Marantz stereo and let the music fill the room. When the song finally trailed off, Steve got up off his recliner and walked toward the stereo. He had a big smile on his face, so naturally I assumed he'd turn up the volume and play the song again. But instead, he ejected the cassette and hiked it between his legs like a football center. It flew up into the air, end over end, until it crashed into the brickwork of his fireplace.

Steve's intentions were always righteous. I knew that, but his tough love was . . . well, it was really tough. I stared at the tape cartridge, now in pieces, and wondered how all my passion and enthusiasm for this song had vanished in less than four seconds. I'm not sure how long it took me to recover from the sound of that cassette crashing into the fireplace, but I assure you, there was a recovery period.

Steven Greenberg (left) and me, 1980

If you're embarking on something new, you must have a strategy in place to protect yourself from the inevitable criticism that will take place when you take your ideas to market. And I'm not necessarily talking about a business marketplace. It could be a fear of communicating honestly in a relationship; it could be about letting someone take a first look at your manuscript or book of poems; it could even be a fear of criticism when discussing party ideas for a friend's birthday.

In the following chapters, we're going to look at ways that I and others have allowed our own Marvs to relax.

Brain Bottle Opener 1: Why You?

Let's start with an easy and incredibly practical tip that I use almost every day:

If you find it hard to begin taking the first steps toward your goal, set a timer for **three minutes**. That way there won't be this daunting glob of time staring you in the face. Three hours is intimidating; three minutes is not. Just start in with whatever small part of your goal you choose. I typically find that when that three-minute alarm goes off, I'm aloft and doing what I was afraid to do just minutes before.

But for now, I'd like you to take no more than **three minutes** to write down the answer to this question: Why are you here? If that's a little too philosophical, try this: What is your purpose in life? If that's too general, then try: What do you stand for? Or:

What would you give your life for? Or: What's the reason you get up in the morning? Or even: What would you want your friends and family to say about who you are?

You might not think a book about unleashing your creative potential has much to do with these big questions, but I believe answering them, or beginning to answer them, helps us to reduce our fear of failure, which helps us to take immediate action toward the fulfillment of our dreams. Knowing who you are, what you stand for, and what you will or will not do for fame or fortune gives you strength—strength of character and strength of purpose. That strength is what allows Marv to put down his guard for a while.

After you've written your Why You statement, keep it close at hand, because it'll provide you with impetus and understanding as we move through the various parts of the Big Muse process.

Note: If you give yourself three minutes to try this and can't think of anything to write, can't think of anything that defines your life's purpose, then consider the fact that you *don't know* a very valuable piece of information, something to solve later.

REAL-WORLD APPLICATIONS

Use this BBO before undertaking any large-scale project or decision. For example, let's say you're a young dentist, just married (your wife is a fifth-grade teacher), and you've been offered a job in a new city. You're trying to assess whether to take the offer. Doing a Why You statement will give you a profound source of information to guide you through the decision-making process.

CHAPTER 2

HISTORY'S HEAVY HAND

DISCONNECTING MARV FROM THE PAIN OF YOUR PAST

When I was twelve years old I was the lead guitar player of a four-piece rock band. We were a miserable group of sixth-graders. But I was the worst of the bunch by far. I was such a malevolent and egomaniacal little prick that once, when I felt our rhythm guitar player, Sean, was making a play for my role as lead, I fomented a conspiracy against him that resulted in every kid in the neighborhood festooning Sean's purple Vox teardrop electric guitar with boogers. In the end it looked like some decoupage project gone entirely wrong.

At the time, I had no idea that my negative thinking was directly proportional to my feelings of fear and vulnerability. How could I have known? I was just a kid, after all. And instead of being self-reflective, perhaps saying to myself, "This is just Marv coming to 'defend' me against a potentially frightening situation," which, of course, would have demanded a level of maturity I simply didn't possess, I did cruel and stupid things to make myself feel stronger.

A short while after the booger incident, our band performed at the Peter Hobart Elementary School Spring Concert. We played so well, in fact, that we immediately secured our first professional engagement: five dollars for the whole band and all the orange pop and Doritos we could stomach. But I was nervous. The gig was at United Cerebral Palsy of Minnesota, and aside from my other moral shortcomings, I had this terrible habit of laughing uncontrollably at the misfortunes of others. If someone was to trip and get hurt, or if a waitress was to drop a tray of dishes, I'd find that hysterical. I was afraid that I'd take one look at these physically challenged people and laugh at them too.

The first person we saw that night in Saint Paul had hydrocephalus, water on the brain. His head was so disturbingly elongated that to my twelve-year-old mind, it looked like a flesh-colored stovepipe hat. A woman who had no hands was drawing a landscape with a green crayon fixed between her toes. A pretty teenage girl, who seemed perfectly normal, except that she had only one layer of skin, was standing near the stage. We could see her dark veins as clearly as we saw her eyes. When we finally started to play, the crowd went wild. The guy with hydrocephalus was rocking back and forth so hard I thought his wheelchair was going to break. The woman with no hands was clapping to the music by pounding her feet on the table, and the girl with one layer of skin was dancing just in front of the band.

We only had six songs, so we kept playing them over and over, until something incredible happened. I suddenly became aware that the voices of fear in my head (the same ones that had made me so defensive that I'd laugh at people's misfortunes and foment booger conspiracies) had vanished. It was like a wave of calm had emptied out my mind. And in that space—that fearless nothing, if you will—I suddenly felt a sense of pure joy as all my self-critical words melted away. Though I hadn't yet given him a name, I was already beginning to feel what it was like when Marv gets up and goes away.

Me (left) and the band, 1972

Not only did I not laugh at anyone, that evening in Saint Paul was the first time I remember experiencing a real sense of purpose. I was bringing joy to people and being made joyful in return. When I looked over at the other guys in the band I could tell they felt it too. On the way home, I realized something in me had shifted. I was too young to adequately express the feeling, but it was somehow clear to me: Acting in the moment, acting generously, and doing what I love to do is how I can get Marv to leave me alone.

FEARLESS NOTHING

A few years ago I read W. H. Auden's poem "In Memory of W. B. Yeats." One line in particular, "poetry makes nothing happen," caught my attention. Auden had written the poem in tribute to his mentor Yeats in 1940, at the dawn of WWII. The words made perfect sense. How could any poem, any piece of music, any painting, or any simple act of kindness, which is its own kind of poetry, possibly stand up to mass murderers and tyrannical governments?

But days later, when I looked at the line again as "poetry makes *nothing* happen," it began to take on an entirely different meaning. In that moment I saw Auden's "nothing" as awareness without fear. I came to believe, and still do, that both great works of art and simple acts of grace allow us a kind of empty space from which to view the world and our lives without preconceptions, without prejudice—a nonjudgmental vantage point—where we can divorce ourselves from tired ways of looking at things and then, and only then, become the truly creative beings we are meant to be. As I understood it, Auden was describing the state of mind from which change of any kind becomes possible. It was then I knew that I needed some practical methods to be able to get space from Marv anytime I desired.

NO MATTER HOW much fear Marv tries to sell us, we should never attempt to banish him or shut him up forever. We treat him with respect because even though he can seem like the most annoying force in our lives, he's always trying his best to be our protector and save us from shame and abandonment. The problem, as we all know, is that he just works way too hard. We may feel like shoving a dirty sock into his mouth but what we really need to do is give him a cup of coffee and a copy of the *New York Times*, and tell him to take a little break. Then while he's away, comfortably sipping his latte and reading the paper, we can do our best work. We need to send him off because the very human impulse to create is so powerful and so much a part of our genetic makeup.

There are some of us who might rightly ask, "Why strive to be creative at all? Maybe life would be better (or easier, at least) if I just sat around watching *Seinfeld* reruns and eating Ben & Jerry's." Fair enough. But my response is that following our dreams isn't just a way to get ahead or to be well liked or to be a productive citizen. Our creativity—that is, our fearless engagement with the world around us—is the source of our happiness and purpose on this planet. Constantly ruminating about what we've achieved in the past or thinking about what results we'll purportedly get in the future has a way of disconnecting us from experiencing that joy. The key to joy is working actively in the present as opposed to constantly being stuck considering outcomes.

Creativity resides in our present-tense efforts to make order from the chaos around us.

*   *   *

THE GREAT PAINTER Georgia O'Keeffe famously said: "I've been absolutely terrified every moment of my life and I've never let it keep me from doing a single thing that I wanted to do." When we take simple, positive actions in spite of our fear, our minds and our possibilities expand. On the other hand, whenever we get wrapped up in negativity, our minds (and our possibilities) contract. The actions we take don't have to be huge or heroic. They might be terribly modest things, like saying thank you to a restaurant server (and meaning it) or making your wife some banana pancakes for the sole reason of seeing her smile. Just as there are specific steps to be taken in the service of our career-oriented dreams, there are specific steps to be taken in the service of the larger dream we all have for ourselves: the dream of one day being happy, impassioned, and fulfilled.

EXPANSION, CONTRACTION, AND THE CURSE OF COMPARISON

At times we become so caught up in the machinations of our daily lives that we forget such a goal is even possible—that happiness is even within the realm of consideration. Our dream might be about starting a business or learning a new language. It could just as easily have to do with seeking out people we long to be with or acting on a desire to deepen our current relationships. As I've said before, every goal is obtainable if we break each one down into individual doable parts, do the actions in the present, and make sure that what we're doing is true to our own values and not something foisted upon us by pressure or control.

You'll notice that a couple of paragraphs back I used the words *expand* and *contract*. I try not to rely on the words *succeed* and *fail*. Too often we're caught up in the trap of thinking in assessment terms. There's finality about succeeding or failing that often doesn't ring true. It's what happens to a character at the end of a book or movie. But life doesn't work that way. It's more nuanced, more ambiguous. We're not coming to the "end" at the end of a day, the end of a job, or even the end of a relationship, though it may well feel as if we are. While we're still alive it's far too early to take a tally or publish a scorecard. Our lives already have way too many assessments. Expansion and contraction are concepts that suggest dynamic states as opposed to dead judgments. They also imply that every situation we find ourselves in (whether that situation goes in our intended direction or not) is in fact just one more learning opportunity.

By choosing to define yourself as a success or a failure, you are also forced into making rigid assessments about your self-worth in comparison to others. If you're not comparing yourself with your friends and neighbors, then you're making comparisons with the fictional characters who pose as humans in magazines and on television. You'll then find that you are constantly anxious about where you "should" be in your life, as opposed to where you *are* in your life.

When we're in the habit of comparing ourselves with everyone around us, it simply means that we've become seduced by the sound of Marv's voice. Instead of sending him away for a few hours, we're sitting at his feet and listening to him as though he's Moses. When we're attentive to him we guarantee one thing: We will be unable to make our dreams manifest.

Here's why:

We are not being specific. We are thinking about our lives as one big insoluble problem and casting a negative light on all of it. If we were taking time to address a small, specific, problematic aspect of our lives and focusing on it alone, as opposed to viewing our entire lives as some giant amorphous ball of chaos and confusion, we could address our challenges in a proactive and creative manner. That's called helpful problem solving—a creative endeavor if ever there was one—as opposed to obsessive thinking over things we can't change.

We are not acting in the present. We have a tendency to think only about the future consequences of our perceived misfortune. We are imagining negative scenarios for ourselves in some distant future in which everything portends gloom and doom.

We are not being true. We're not basing any of our thoughts or actions on things we truly desire. Since we are comparing ourselves and our circumstances to others, we become incapable of looking at our own uniqueness, our own desires, or our own aspirations. Rather, we're being led into some kind of dim reverie of negativity.

We humans are not static, and to speak about our lives in terms of failure or success suggests that we have somehow stopped. The journey of our lives is just that—a journey. We're still in process, still in motion. I prefer to ask, "Does the course of action I've taken at any given moment expand my potential, both in terms of a particular goal and my overall happiness, or does it contract the possibilities?"

I'm also suspicious about the value of constantly declaring

what we are. Sometimes we give ourselves proud appraisals: I'm an artist, a dentist, a research scientist. Other times we label ourselves negatively: I'm not creative, not outgoing, not disciplined. The weight of these kinds of pronouncements and the energy we expend attaching ourselves to them are only limiting. I'm aware that we have some evolutionary need to make snap determinations about one another (who's liberal, who's conservative, who's got the heft of academic or professional success behind them and who doesn't . . .). Sure, we love our name tags, but the problem is that we don't just wear them; we often believe that we *are* them.

Whether we're proud of our identities or degraded by them, the names we give ourselves should never be mistaken for who we are. What truly define us are our core values—the ideas, the conversations, and the actions we engage in. Simply put, those things must be nurtured if they expand our minds (and the minds of others) and rejected if they contract them.

The Zen tradition teaches that at our core, each of us is just an observer. We are not what we've achieved or what we own. We are simply the consciousness that looks out at the world from behind our senses. When we lose ourselves in the storm of negative emotions stirred by our senses, when we lose knowledge of ourselves as simply observers, we surrender our ability to act with freedom and creativity. We become, in a sense, slaves to Marv.

ELEPHANT ROPES AND THE ABRASIONS THEY CAUSE

In India, elephant handlers train baby elephants to be submissive by chaining them to a post. The baby elephants fight with all their will to break free. Day in and day out they try, but eventually they just give up. When they become adults they no longer need chains to tie them in place; just a thin rope will do. Of course an adult elephant, with its tremendous strength, is perfectly capable of breaking the rope, but since its experiences as a baby have convinced it otherwise, it never tries. This is how some circus trainers keep elephants captive.

In many ways we're not much different from those elephants. Our own painful past experiences are capable of limiting us in a similar fashion, and it's worth taking a look at some of the ropes each of us has tied around our own ankles. Being aware of what these look and feel like is important. The more we know about the causes of our own fear, the less ground Marv has to stand on and the less convincing his arguments will be. But looking at a memory that has created our "Elephant Ropes" can be frightening, especially for people who have suffered crippling emotional, physical, or sexual abuse.

When I think back on the Elephant Rope breakthroughs I've made over the years—moments of discovery when I realized just how I'd been fooling myself into thinking I was trapped or chained—I'm always amazed at the innocence behind the experiences. I mean, we've all had traumatic moments in our lives of some sort, and yes, those moments can certainly become Elephant Ropes, but more often than not, the ropes that are the most constraining and damaging are ridiculously subtle. They stay just under the radar—they have to, or else we'd recognize the illusion and they'd lose their power.

As you will see, many of the examples I draw on from my past in helping to explain Marv and his sneaky ways of stifling our creativity are from my childhood. There are two good reasons I like to go back to my early years. The first is that creativity takes place in the mind of a child. "I'm an adult," you say. Yes, but even so, your childlike mind is still very much a part of you, although clearly, for many that childlike mind has become difficult to access. The second reason is that shame has its root in innocence, and shining a light on Marv's toolbox usually requires traveling back in our childhoods to those naive moments of an Elephant Rope's first weaving.

AN ELEPHANT ROPE OF MINE

I remember one such incident in the late summer of 1972. It was a scary time for me. Soon I'd be going to junior high and meeting all sorts of new kids. I wasn't good at sports, and in Minnesota everyone played either football or hockey. The girls seemed to really be attracted to the jocks, with their shoulder pads and hockey sticks, and I felt like I'd never be able to compete for their attention. One afternoon, my parents were gone for the day and I called the guys in my band and asked them to come over for a rehearsal. We set up in the garage and started running through our songs. After a while the music was sounding so good we opened the garage door so everyone in the neighborhood could hear.

Twenty minutes later, small groups of kids started walking over to watch us—kids from other elementary schools who'd be going to my junior high a month from then. It was exciting, and pretty soon the trickle of kids had grown to a crowd, including some really cute girls I'd heard about but never actually met. To my good fortune our rehearsal had turned into a full-blown rock concert, and after we'd played for an hour or so, all the guys, who were getting very rowdy, started filing into my house and into the basement.

It was then that I blasted an 8-track of Jimi Hendrix through my brother's enormous speakers, which lit up in different colors to the beat of the music. I started going wild and whipped off my tank top, spraying my underarms with a can of Right Guard in perfect time to Jimi's guitar solo. I thought it was hilarious and all the guys were playing air guitars with orgasmic expressions on their faces. All I could think about was how great I felt and how popular I'd be with all these new kids in the fall when school started.

When we finally went outside to cool off, there was a group of incredibly cute girls in my driveway. There they were—at my house! This was the moment I'd been waiting for. These girls were going to fawn over me. To this day, I can still remember feeling supremely confident as I walked toward them. And then the record-scratching moment of panic as one dark-haired girl named Janelle suddenly blurted out, "Himmelman, you're so immature. You're not even ready for seventh grade." No one came to my rescue. Janelle's foxy friends just nodded in agreement. Worst of all—Marv nodded in agreement, and an Elephant Rope slipped firmly around my leg for, oh, I'd say a good twenty years or more.

Cue the sad violas and the lonely oboe. . . .

Today, looking back on that moment, I don't see a loser at all. I see an incredibly creative and interesting kid who was doing something entirely different from what anyone going into Westwood Junior High was doing. I had my own band. We were playing my original songs. I was into Jimi Hendrix and I was daring and funny enough to spray deodorant on my underarms as a percussion instrument. I'd love that kid if I met him today. As I think about Janelle and what she'd said, I wonder why I didn't just stare her

down and say, "What do you know about maturity? You're twelve."
As it turned out, Marv had seized on that moment and had said:

> Peter, I told you not to do weird things. No one's gonna under-
> stand your sense of humor and no one cares about you or your
> music. So please, don't embarrass yourself anymore. Just try to
> be quiet and fit in this fall, okay? Seventh grade's a big deal and
> you've really blown it today.

Brain Bottle Opener 2: Elephant Ropes

Take **five minutes** to discover and write about one of your own Elephant Ropes. The more you know about the causes of your own fear, the less ground Marv has to stand on, and the less his arguments will remain convincing.

An Elephant Rope could be something as seemingly insignificant as your father telling you to stop making so much "goddamn noise" when you were singing in the backseat of the car. (A note to parents: It takes only one incident like that to shut down a lifetime of singing.)

Describe this experience with as much detail as five minutes will allow (the more particulars, the better). Sights, sounds, smells, dates, times . . . all of it. Be as descriptive as possible.

REAL-WORLD APPLICATIONS

This BBO is particularly helpful when you have a goal in mind that you just can't seem to find the time to act on. What you're feeling is fear, not a crisis of time management. It's your Elephant Ropes that are making the goal seem way more daunting than it actually is. Let's say, for example, that you want to deepen your relationship with your older sister. You really want to call her but it's been a while, you've had some difficulty communicating with her in the past, and you're not sure how the conversation will go. You're thinking that you need time to make this happen—a large block of time, perhaps—that you don't currently have. I want to remind you, the call has nothing to do with time; it has to do with Marv setting up emotional roadblocks. Do this BBO and see how your perspective changes.

CHAPTER 3

A MAN IN MARV'S GRIP

THE MANY WAYS WE FOOL OURSELVES

My cousin and longtime bandmate Jeff Victor is a musical genius. Understand that I'm very judicious with the g-word. I don't bring it out often and when I do, it's only for the sake of precision, not flattery or hyperbole. As musicians' minds go, Jeff's doesn't merely melodize or harmonize; it orchestrates. His mind churns so fast and so consistently overflows with musical ideas that it disturbs his sleep. He's a pianist and a tremendous singer, and he composes songs and instrumental music. He also happens to be one of the funniest people I've ever met. Jeff's dream is to perform a concert of his original music. He's been a sideman forever, playing keyboards with dozens of local and national acts, but it's been more than thirty years since he's played his own music onstage. His dream is nothing huge, at least not to me. It's just a club date in his hometown of Minneapolis. Or is it?

Here's the problem: He can't seem to "just do it." He tells me he doesn't have the time, the self-discipline, or the drive. Maybe that's true, but I don't believe any of those things. I think he's lying to himself.

I think Marv's got him cornered.

No doubt there would be some work needed on his part and a few logistical things to take care of before a Jeff Victor show actually materialized. But I assure you, there's nothing earth-shattering stopping him—just a few small actions to be taken in the present. Here's what he'd need to do:

- Select some pieces of music, maybe ten or twelve, to perform a set (he's got dozens of pieces of music).
- Rehearse with a band (he knows all sorts of excellent players who would play with him in a heartbeat).
- Contact a club owner or local promoter (he knows everyone in town and he's very popular in the Minneapolis music scene).
- Pick a performance date and alert some friends and fans.
- And finally: He'd need to sit his butt down on the piano bench and play the concert.

If you look at this list, perhaps you're struck, as I am, at the ridiculously easy path that connects Jeff and his dream. It's not as though he wants to become a doctor and perform open-heart surgery in his own medical reality show. Or if you prefer: He's not planning the Jeff Victor World Tour with a dozen semis, two tour buses, and a backup choir. It's just a gig at a club in his hometown. Jeff simply dreams of doing something that's literally a phone call away. So why is it that he can't make this happen? What has Marv said to him and why is it so compelling? So constricting? So controlling?

As we'll see, Marv has Jeff ensnared in a clever distraction that's short on content but long on stifling contentment.

TOPS ON THE TO-DO LIST: MAKE A TO-DO LIST

Here's something about Jeff that's interesting to note: He's a compulsive list maker and planner. He'll make handwritten lists of things he needs to accomplish. Things like:

Pack underwear for trip
Buy new toothpaste
Find blue sweater
Call Dad about snow blower
Make sure ice trays aren't leaking
Buy new blades for electric shaver
Sell Vox Jaguar electric organ
Return green plastic rake to Target
Get extra hose for backyard
Take vitamin D tablets
Buy Paul Mitchell shampoo for oily hair
Pack dress socks

Jeff's lists illustrate the frenzied minutiae of his daily life. What's more, the list items never get finished from day to day—and they start to accumulate until this great heap of hundreds of things that can never get done morphs into a small mountain on his desk. But it's more than just paper. It's become a testament that proves (to Jeff, at least) that it's impossible to truly accomplish anything resembling a dream.

Yet are the lists simply how he avoids actually doing anything, while convincing himself he's doing something? They are specific (unbearably specific) but they're not present or true. There's nothing about the items on the list that forces the tasks to get completed or even started in the present (many of the items on the lists are months old). Worst of all, they're all things he can push off to sometime in the near or distant future. There's also nothing in the reams of chores that suggests any of them reflect Jeff's true aspirations. Now stop and reflect: How often have you cleaned out a file cabinet or e-mail inbox, or organized a sock drawer, while something of far greater significance goes neglected?

Nothing in a Jeff Victor list alludes to his desire to perform a concert, for example. Nothing relates to anything he is actually passionate about! These bullet points of busywork exist only to distract him from doing what he truly wants to do—but truly fears doing. Keep in mind: Jeff is an incredibly accomplished pianist, composer, and arranger. And once, when he was young, he boasted enough patience and passion to get those incredibly complex skills under his belt in the first place.

Jeff started playing piano in earnest around eighth grade. Where was Marv then? How come he couldn't stop Jeff from learning to play the piano? Why didn't Jeff quit through the hours of grueling lessons and repetitive practice drills? And what happened to Jeff in later years that prevents him from doing something we'd all regard as pretty simple, at least for a talented musician: putting on a performance? To put a fine point on it: When and why did Jeff stop listening to the music in his mind and in his heart and start listening to Marv? And how did Jeff forget his creative identity, so much so that in terms of his own simple dream, this prodigious talent no longer thinks of himself as Jeff Victor but as Jeff Loser?

A TALE OF LOVE AND FEAR

I asked Jeff what he loves about creating music, and he described how it makes him feel calm, "in a place beyond confidence—a state of pure being." He'd started taking lessons when he was five, but he didn't like to read music. What he found was that he could listen to his teacher play, come back the next week, and play the piece by ear perfectly. It wasn't discipline that was driving him to practice—it was sheer love of the instrument. By his own admission, he had no discipline whatsoever. He loved to sing as he played, and the more he sang and played, the more he started to recognize relationships from one chord to the next, and how it made him feel. He started to appreciate chords and harmony. He just loved how his fingers felt on the keys.

In telling his story, not once did he mention a word about lists or time management.

When I finally got to the million-dollar question of how he felt about doing his solo show, I could feel him bouncing clear out of his comfort zone. His breathing and his body language changed. It was as if he'd physically tightened. There was a palpable hesitation in his voice as he stammered, "I feel very confident . . . umm, I mean, with the slight hesitation, of . . . well, more than slight hesitation about my vocals."

Then when I asked him about his level of drive to perform the show, he just looked out the window and stared for a while before answering. "If a ten is 'I will not let anything get in my way—not money, not sleep, not family,' and a one is 'I don't have any desire—like, if I die and don't play this show I won't regret not having done it,' I would say I'm probably at around a five."

To me, all that calculating sounded like Jeff was simply afraid—afraid no one would like his show, afraid no one would like him. And when I asked him about it he agreed. "Look," he told me, "if I knew it would be enormously successful, I'd drop just about everything I'm currently doing. I'd do a lot of things differently if I knew I'd be an enormous success."

Think about that statement for a moment. We'd all like to eliminate fear before we try something new. When we were young we felt fear, but somehow it didn't stop us. There wasn't a clear point where it was simply gone. We had a fear but we'd just do what we wanted anyway. We've all been there. We've all felt that sort of impervious childlike innocence, and then somewhere along the line it goes missing, and it feels like something we can't regain—a paradise lost. Ask yourself what happened to your own childlike sense of belief in your ability to make your dreams manifest. Our run-ins with failure (contraction) have given us a surplus of caution.

We've somehow internalized the idea that the reward for following our dreams is not adequate compensation for the pain we experience when things don't work out as we hoped they would. But is this conclusion something we've arrived at with true deliberation or is it some subconscious non-decision?

I asked Jeff, "If you were to take a first step toward playing a concert, what would it be?" That's when he launched into this somewhat convoluted explanation:

"I drew up a list of twelve songs a while ago, which I can't seem to find. Maybe they're in storage; I dunno. Well, I'll probably need to give some thought as to how I'd pull it all off technically too. Let's say I have recordings that I'd like to use as backing tracks to reproduce what's on my CDs. For example, how many people to have in the band? Or do I have to do it alone? Or wait—maybe there'd be, like, twelve musicians onstage. . . . Do I play all instrumental music or do I sing or . . . ?"

Can you hear how confusing Jeff is making things? There's nothing specific about what he's just told me. There isn't any clear first goal. And when you're looking to accomplish a goal, that kind of confusion is where the trouble usually starts.

"Jeff, can you give me just a tiny first step?" I asked. "One small piece that you can do to move this along? Something you can do in five minutes or less?"

He looked at me and said, "You mean what I said just now wasn't small?"

In fact it wasn't small or specific. It was all over the place and it was very confusing.

In Jeff's case, an example of a small step I'm looking for would be to take five minutes to find that missing list of songs, or if he can't find it, to sit down and write a new one. Either one would constitute a small, specific, and actionable step. But then, as if not hearing a word I'd said, he dove straight back into unnecessary complexity. "Okay, okay," he agreed, "that makes sense; I get it. But now, how am I gonna do these songs? Am I gonna use tape-backing synced up to the live music mixed together to create a big sound that I enjoy, or should I pare it down? Who am I gonna call to play these songs and how much are they gonna charge me?" That's when I felt I needed to jump in and give Jeff some more concrete examples of what these small steps look and feel like. If you don't know what to look for, you won't ever find it.

One other specific and actionable idea would be for Jeff to give himself ten minutes to go through each song on his list (once he's found it or rewritten it) and think about a possible sound for each song, to think about what might be best for him in terms of arrangement or style.

It might look something like this (excuse my ridiculous made-up titles):

"Reaction Ninety-one"—*do this as an up-tempo rocker*
"Buttercup Deliverance"—*slow ballad style*
"Mrs. Pemmingway's Hat"—*solo piano*
"Metallurgical Mistake"—*hard rock*
"Drowning in Sand"—*definitely Americana rock*

Jeff thought for a while and I could feel the wheels of his prodigious brain turning. "None of what you're saying is difficult," he finally said. "I'm just worried I don't have the time."

Time—that lamest of justifications . . . Although merely thinking about a possible musical choice for each of the twelve songs would happen almost instantaneously for a musician as skilled as Jeff, I wasn't surprised to hear him obfuscating what should normally be a very simple process by pulling out the classic time excuse. And so he continued in the same sort of muddled vein. I was averse to interrupting, but I asked him how long it would take just to think of a possible musical direction, and he told me what I'd already known: "It would take two seconds per song."

I knew then that Jeff understood exactly the point I'd been trying to make: our not being able to pursue our ideas is almost never about a lack of time. It's all about Marv and his eloquent expressions of fear.

And when you want to accomplish a goal, you can't wait around for Marv to suddenly become fearless. In fact, he never will until *you take action*. Jeff needed to bring the concert into existence by picking something he could actually do in a very short time. Start there. Even if what that amounted to was only planning for the future. That was something he agreed he could do.

"Here's the thing," I said to him. "I think you're absolutely terrified of doing this concert. Instead of just admitting that you're afraid, you're creating all this confusion so that you'll never have to be on the hook for actually having to do this concert. You're making it so difficult it'll never happen."

He looked up at me. "Yeah," he said, "I guess I don't think I'm good enough."

FEEDBACK, FEAR, AND REFRAMING: WHAT JEFF'S STORY CAN TEACH US

We'll come back to Jeff Victor in a bit, but for now, let's distill a few lessons from his experience to use on our creative journeys. As we do this, let's resist the temptation to label or judge him. That wouldn't help him—or us—to realize prized dreams.

Obviously Jeff needs less rumination and more action. He's also allowed Marv to turn rain puddles into raging seas. But Jeff is honest enough to admit that he's afraid and confused. It's an insidious cycle. His confusion leads to fear, which feeds his confusion, which multiplies his fear, and so on.

Let's outline three steps that could help him gain some clarity.

Reframing: Jeff has to go back to the very beginning as though dreaming the concert for the first time. Whatever his roadblocks or objections, he has a chance to start over and reframe things. As he correctly surmised, he must ask himself, "How bad do I want this show?" But now he needs to ask himself this question as if nothing's standing in his way, and as if he's never been blocked about it. He needs to wipe the slate clean before reconsidering whether the dream of doing a show still holds appeal. That's crucial. If he asks the question from his current perspective, Marv will cut him off with thirty years' worth of ready-made excuses.

Reinforcement: Now Jeff needs enticement and excitement. Rather than *think* (the left brain's specialty), he needs to *dream* (the right brain's specialty). To do that, he must let go and visualize himself onstage at the show: What will this look and sound like? Can he see the smiling faces and hear the enthusiastic applause? Who's playing with him? This imagined scene is the beginning of Jeff's being able to *see his dream* in a positive light.

Reporting: People who try to lose weight or exercise in a gym know it goes much better when they have a workout partner or a spotter. Maybe Jeff needs just such a spotter, or coach, to check in with as he breaks the dream into action steps. Having someone to hold him accountable will help him keep focused on things that matter—and set aside distractions that don't.

Once Jeff has these steps accomplished, he needs to break the Elephant Rope for good with these three additional actions:

Regroup: Now Jeff might expand his circle with musicians who are positive and supportive, who will encourage him to press on toward the mark. At this point Jeff needs to get himself into a room, playing his music with people who love his work. The dream is feeling more real all the time.

Reality check: Set a due date. The positive pressure of a due date does two things. First, it reminds Jeff's fearful self—his Marv—that this "woolly mammoth" will go away by a certain date and time. And second: It creates more positive pressure for Jeff to focus on what matters, to get ready for the show.

Reassurance: Don't sweat the outcome. Jeff Victor knows how to let go as a musician. As he said, "I get calm; I'm somewhere in a place beyond confidence. I'm not trying to do anything. I'm being." What Jeff is relating is that sense of fearless nothing that I described in the previous chapter. It's the perfect exemplar of Auden's line: "poetry makes *nothing* happen." He needs to have a similar detachment in regard to his perfectionism—wanting to play the perfect set with the perfect songs and the perfect musical cast—and treat the set as equal parts experiment and experience.

Finally, Jeff needs leverage. Marv will try to bully him at every step. But there's an old proverb that says, "The one thing the devil can't stand is being mocked." If Jeff can laugh at himself, and treat the destination for what it is—just one concert on one day in his life—his demons will shrink away. Being aware, truly aware, of Marv and his antics is the first step in disempowering him. If Jeff had even a trace of objectivity, he'd find the whole thing more hilarious than intimidating. By getting and staying specific, present, and true, Jeff Victor can finally concentrate not on the nightmares, but on living out his dream concert.

Let's see what life would look like for him if he were free to pursue what he truly loves. When I asked Jeff what a brilliant performance in which people stood up and clapped for him would feel like, he had this to say:

"It'd feel fantastic. I would have unrivaled sex with my wife, I would be more funny, more creative and lighthearted with my children, and I would be motivated to do a lot more music performances. It would put me on a high, an unparalleled high. I would turn into the best version of myself I could possibly imagine."

For those of you looking for a postscript to Jeff's story, you should know that he made his dream come true on a wintry Saturday night, opening for another musician at a small club in Excelsior, Minnesota. He'd taken a Specific, Present, and True approach, and instead of being incapacitated with anxiety, as he had been when he was just thinking about the project, he followed his goal through to completion. It was as if Marv's negative voice had entirely disappeared.

Not only was Jeff's playing and singing amazing (as I knew it would be), he reported: "Being onstage was like entering a portal where everything was pure joy and possibility." The hour-and-fifteen-minute performance passed without his even noticing it. In his words: "I've never felt so happy and free in all my life."

Brain Bottle Opener 3: Marv's Furlough Notice

Take **three minutes** to write a note to Marv that tells him why you're going to be sending him on regular, daily vacations. It could sound something like this:

Dear Marv,

You're a great guy and I want you to know that I appreciate everything you've been doing for me all these years. All the protection you've provided me has been an invaluable addition to my well-being. In consideration of all that, I'm going to allow you much more free time. I'm going to be doing [name your dream] from now on and I want you to know that I'll be okay. Please save your strength for times when I really need it. For example, should I ever fall from the deck of an ocean liner, please help me scream (and swim). And if I ever find myself being chased by a puma, please help me run. But unless those kinds of things should happen, please feel free to lounge about all day. Eat, read, go for a walk—whatever it is you need to do, now is the time to do it. Okay?

Your friend,
Peter

REAL-WORLD APPLICATIONS

This BBO is perfect for those times when you feel a lack of confidence. When you break your dream into small, specific parts that are practical and doable, confidence becomes a totally irrelevant factor. For example, let's say you want to learn to play the piano. A small (really small but important), specific step would be to look up the names of piano teachers in your area and check out their references. This does not require some special skill. Doing Marv's Furlough Notice is a good way to gain impetus to engage in that simple step.

CHAPTER 4

MEET THE DEFLATORS

THE CHALLENGE CONTINUES...

Have you ever noticed that the stories we tell ourselves to deflect from acting on our dreams are actually highly creative? They've got great hooks, nuanced character development, breathtaking cinematography, and incredible dialogue. It's almost as if Marv has a team of brilliant filmmakers at his disposal—let's call them the Deflators—whose primary goal is to engage our imagination for the sole purpose of discouraging our imagination. Talk about irony.

The moment we get serious about a dream, Marv calls an emergency production meeting with the Deflators. Here are some notes from their production meeting back when I was getting started with Big Muse:

Look, Deflators, I'm afraid Peter's going to get himself into some serious trouble with this Big Muse idea of his. I need you guys to get busy with a movie we can project on the screen of his consciousness. We can even play the thing as he sleeps, but it's got to be convincing. It's got to make him understand that this business will fail and he needs to see how much harm the failure's gonna bring him. We've gotta put him in touch with some of his most vulnerable childhood emotions.

And here's an example of a little movie magic the Deflators put together for me. It was made of footage from when I was in first grade.

It's winter. I'm walking home from the bus stop carrying a math quiz with one of the answers wrong. The incorrect answer represents the chance, however small, that my parents could stop loving me. I reason that if I'm not perfect, I might be left alone to freeze out here. My survival instinct kicks in. When I'm sure there's no one looking, I crush the paper into a ball and push it deep into the snowbank with the heel of my boot.

In all fairness to my parents, I can't exactly say where those ideas came from. Maybe from fairy tales I'd read, maybe from some Disney movie (lots of traumatic stuff in those things), but the point is that those fears I experienced felt real. They actually caused me to lie and to hide the source of my shame, regardless of the fact that there wasn't a chance in hell I'd actually be rejected by my parents, let alone cast out into a Minnesota winter's night. But there you have it—the Deflators created a little cinematic gem, which on some hidden emotional level said, "Don't be less than perfect or you might die."

These kinds of negative thoughts are very seductive, and without some means of interdiction, they have a way of slowly draining the air out of your dreams. You need to be aware of how your own mind works and catch yourself before you get too far down the negativity track as you begin working on an idea. Recalling the Zen tradition I mentioned earlier, maintaining a sense of being an observer—that is, being able to relax and see what's happening around you without falling into a stew of raw emotions—is key. One trick you can do anytime and anywhere to relax your mind is to take three very deep, very slow breaths. Try slowly breathing in through your nose and out through pursed lips as though you were exhaling through a straw. I find myself doing this several times during the day and it works wonders. When you are relaxed you can begin to bear witness to how your mind works. By maintaining a calm objectivity you stay free to act in the moment.

But beware: Oftentimes the more creative we get, the more creative the Deflators get. If we can stop and see them for what they really are, then we can enlist them in producing the movie we want to see.

THE ANCIENT GREEKS understood this concept. In the story of Orestes, the Furies are three monsters who attack and terrify Orestes day and night with their relentless criticism and ghoulish appearance, all because of a little family drama involving pride and murder (nothing like a little family dysfunction to get those Furies hopping mad).

Only when Orestes takes responsibility for his actions at a trial held by the gods do the Furies transform into "fairies," or Eumenides, that guide Orestes as wise, loving spirits. Thousands of years old, this myth speaks volumes about the most basic creative dilemma of all: Do we succumb to the voices that haunt us or do we take accountability for our lives and dreams and take action? Even though they were vexing, Orestes didn't angrily banish the Furies. He accepted personal responsibility, reflected on the Furies' positive virtues, and only then were they transformed into wise guides.

We break the cycle when we recognize what's taking place in our minds—when we understand that the negative feelings that crop up to quell our dreams are really the products of our own fruitful imaginations. We need only begin to take the small actions toward our goals to break away from the negativity. When we do that, we change the Deflators' directives and orientation. Then they immediately bring their awesome skills and come to work for us.

DESIGNING A DREAM

Meet Andy Cruz, a talented graphic designer and illustrator. He's made a nice living for himself working in the advertising industry in Los Angeles. In the past several years, the economics of producing images have undergone seismic shifts because of the abundance of excellent and inexpensive design software that allows almost anyone to create professional-looking layouts and graphics. As a result, Andy's job, his sense of himself, and the direction he knows he needs to go next have been trod upon. Some days he maintains a clear vision of just what he needs to do to make a change; other days it all seems so confusing.

Andy is afraid he might lose his job. He figures he has eight months to a year before it ends, but he hasn't yet begun to seriously look elsewhere. He's put "feelers" out, inquired about similar positions, but he hasn't shifted into action mode. What he really needs, he says, is a business plan to get organized—something he's never really done before. So I asked him to describe what this business might look like:

"I don't see it as too much different from what I'm doing now, doing custom design and illustration for clients and having a big, nice library of stuff to license to people. But I keep asking myself, Am I really good enough? Is it current? Is it going to touch somebody emotionally?"

I was curious why Andy had such a negative attitude. He called it a function of his personality. When he's "in a kind of in-between place," as he puts it, he's far more susceptible to feeling like no one's going to value his work. When I asked him if he'd shown his new stuff to anyone, even a single person, he told me exactly what I'd expected: "Not a soul."

How many times growing up have you heard the phrase "You can't know unless you try"? How is it that we often feel we know with certainty that we're not good enough? When you see someone—a friend, your spouse, or a child—rationalizing his or her own inaction, it's so often obviously illogical. But when it's *you*, a 100 percent negative outcome is the sanest thing you've ever heard.

Consider this: How many times in your life has an answer to a question boiled down to making contact, making a phone call? What stops you from the simple act of dialing?

I wondered how Andy would feel if instead of thinking about all the possible ways he could fail, he just took it upon himself to call someone he'd worked with successfully in the past, simply dialed ten digits that afternoon. "What would it be like," I asked, "if you got a positive response like, 'Hey, yeah, let's meet early for lunch next week'?" For Andy, the answer was easy. "That would definitely give me hope," he said. I also wondered if he felt there was a good chance someone would want to meet with him. As I anticipated, Andy brightened a bit and said, "Yeah, of course. I'm almost ninety-five percent certain I could get at least one of my past clients on the phone."

A moment before, Andy was so certain of what the results would be if he tried reaching out to one of his past clients that he didn't even see the point in bothering. How did the number go from 100 percent negative to 95 percent positive? Let's focus on the positive a little longer.

I asked Andy to think a bit more about how a yes might change his outlook—to imagine the lunch or the setup to the lunch and how he might begin to think about pitching the idea of working for a past client if he knew a meeting was imminent. To that he said, "If I had a good response to my request for the meeting, it would be a complete change for the better."

Now, I'll bet you're thinking exactly what I was thinking: "It seems so simple—just shut the hell up and call the guy!" But as it always does when Marv is steering the ship, what should be simple becomes complicated. Instead of moving forward with a task as easy as dialing up a satisfied past client, Andy's fear took over. See if the confusion he's sowing in this next paragraph sounds the least bit familiar:

"One of the people that I'd love to call just got a new position in San Francisco, but he's so high up in the company he probably doesn't even have anything to do with finding a new illustrator or anything like that. I'm not sure he's even the right guy to be speaking with at this point. I wonder if he'd even remember me. Hmm . . . maybe I should call this one guy who used to know him and he could sort of reintroduce us. But then, I don't even know where to find that guy anymore. . . ."

This is a perfect example of *complexity in place of simplicity*. It's Marv's stock-in-trade.

At that point I put my hand on Andy's shoulder to sort of ease him out of his fear trance. And in a quiet, steady voice I said, "Look, just call the guy. Call him, book a flight, and get the hell up there."

It was as if a bell had rung inside Andy's head. "You know," he said, "I've been way overthinking this. My relationship with him is actually pretty solid—not like best buddies or anything, but it's good enough that if I were to say, 'Hey, I'm going to be in town on this day, is there any way that we could grab a lunch or a coffee?' I know he'd be up for it. In fact, I'm a hundred percent certain that even if the guy's super busy he'd be willing to give me twenty minutes for a cup of coffee."

Now Andy's gone from a 95 percent expected success rate to 100 percent. When you look at your situation as this huge, nebulous blob of confusion and doubt and fear, you will invariably feel as if you can't achieve your goals. Negativity thrives in that confusion. But when you start to punch in those ten numbers, make that call, take that action—whatever it may be—the fear naturally abates.

I could hear the tone in Andy's voice lighten as he contemplated the implications of this simple act—dialing a series of ten numbers—and how it could really change everything about the way he was looking at his future. The simplicity of the action is key, because it doesn't give fear time to impose itself. Once the meeting is set, you're already marshaling your resources; those images you need to get together, that portfolio of artwork, rewriting your résumé, compiling case studies or architectural renderings—whatever they are, you will get them together.

Postscript to Andy's story: While he didn't end up connecting with his contact in San Francisco, three weeks after my conversation with him, Andy e-mailed a friend who'd recently taken a job at a media company in the San Fernando Valley. That e-mail led to his scheduling a meeting with the friend's boss, which led to Andy compiling a portfolio of his older and more current work. There was a good fit and I'm happy to report that Andy is now working as part of a select team of designers creating online marketing materials for Fortune 500 clients.

Brain Bottle Opener 4: Fear-Reduction Benefits

We know what fear wants you to see. What do you want to see instead? Try this:

Take **three minutes** to write down a list of ways that letting go of some of your fear would positively impact your life.

Don't list external benefits such as fame, wealth, or power. I'm talking about subtle internal benefits. For example, let's say you have a dream of owning your own snowboarding school. How would getting over your fear about finally taking the concrete steps toward owning the snowboarding school affect your overall mood, your sense of self, your relationship with your spouse or your parents?

An internal benefit might read something like this:

Reducing my attention to fear would allow me to create my own snowboarding school. With a thriving business, I would wake up in the morning on the top of that mountain with a strong sense of purpose, knowing that I'm bringing joy to others.

Let's say your goal is to ask your boss for a raise. Your internal benefit might sound something like this:

If I stopped being swept away by my fears, I could finally lay out an argument that would make my boss see why I deserve a raise. I would not only bring in some much-needed extra money, it would make me feel like I was taking more control over my own life. I would feel a greater sense of pride, and that pride would translate to my being able to show more affection to my family.

REAL-WORLD APPLICATIONS

This BBO is particularly useful when you're trying to find the strength to start something that's particularly fearful for you. If you're a teacher and have to deliver an important lecture to your class the next morning, or you have to give a presentation at work in front of your board, creating this list of Fear-Reduction Benefits will help. You will be able to push back against your fear-filled vision and replace it with your own scenario of a positive outcome—one that derives from having more volition and subsequently more power to bring your ideas to fruition.

PART ONE REVIEW

BEFORE WE MOVE forward into the next part of the book, take a moment to reflect on what you have accomplished so far through these four Brain Bottle Openers.

- You have written a Why You letter that boldly states what you believe your life's purpose is. If you were unable to write this, you should know that's good too. Knowing what you don't know is always helpful.
- You have explored one of your Elephant Ropes, an experience from your vulnerable past that holds you back today. Just being aware of what might rightly be considered Marv's main ammunition (your fearful memories) is a way of diminishing his power. You've done just that.
- You've written Marv's Furlough Notice, explaining to him just why you're going to be giving him time off. Look, I know it's just a metaphor—there's not really a guy named Marv in your head (at least, no neuroscientist that I'm aware

of has found him yet)—but what you've done in this BBO
is reinforce your ability to take control of your destiny by
gently (always gently) removing his authority.

- You've made a list of Fear-Reduction Benefits. You create
and maintain a positive state of mind by understanding the
ways your life could change for the better if you were able to
significantly reduce your attention to fear.

Now let's focus on the rewards of minimizing our fear.

PART TWO

THE REWARDS

We're so engaged in doing things to achieve
purposes of outer value that we forget the
inner value, the rapture that is associated with
being alive, is what it is all about.

−Joseph Campbell

CHAPTER 5

THE TASTE OF VICTORY

MILKY WAY MOMENTS EXPLAINED

Okay, it's time for slightly odd metaphors. Stay with me. Imagine that your boundless joy—the kind you get when you sense that your life overflows with endless possibilities—is like the unfathomable reaches of the Milky Way galaxy. Picture the heavens, majestic with white-hot stars, each of them shining on you and your dreams for a brighter future. You are aloft, weightless, impossibly free-spirited, and brimming with hope. Or . . . if astronomy isn't your thing, then let's imagine that same boundless joy as a gigantic

Milky Way candy bar. Picture that sucker. It's huge, maybe twelve feet long, three feet wide, and two feet tall. It's laid out on some enormous picnic table and it represents the kind of ecstasy I just described: all chocolate, caramel, and pure unfettered creative nougat. That's the kind of exquisite gratification you get as soon as you become engrossed in the small actions that make the manifestation of a dream possible. I call that feeling a Milky Way Moment.

Let's say that becoming a world-class musician is your goal. Now imagine you're a kid and you play the violin. You have a vision of yourself playing Carnegie Hall one day. Here's the thing about Milky Way Moments: You don't get them only when you make it to Carnegie Hall (after fifteen years of grueling practice and a good bit of luck); you get them *the moment you become engaged in the experience*—in this case, the experience of making music. The Milky Way Moment could happen while you're practicing by yourself. It could happen when you're carried away listening to Jascha Heifetz playing Paganini's Caprice no. 24, or it could happen at a performance for your eighth-grade student body. The size of the venue doesn't make any difference. If you're consumed by the experience of making music, your body and mind will go through the same sensations whether you're playing for twelve people at your local church or that dream gig at Carnegie Hall. Engaging in the small steps of bringing your dream into focus is what brings you to your Milky Way Moment. This is true no matter what your dream is.

That's not to say that thinking about monetary compensation, improved social status, or whatever reward you might want to accrue from a certain goal is a bad thing. But the very human need to experience a sense of accomplishment is the essence of the Milky Way Moment, and we achieve that feeling when we go from the anxious mulling to the active doing. When we participate in simple actions rather than worried considerations, we gain a sense of comfort in seeing that we've finally shown some agency and taken some control. That's when Marv can become an ally—a mix of Jung's golden shadow and a benevolent critic—helping us polish our nascent efforts until they shine.

Take Andrea Kern, from Pasadena, California. Thirty-two years old and married with one daughter, she recently got her real estate license and has long wanted to start a blog on the best way to sell a home in her area. Today, she decided to make that small goal a reality. Here's what she did:

- 9:25 A.M.: She called a friend and said, "Hey, I'm starting my blog this morning."
- 9:30 A.M.: She went online and started reading some blogs from other writers for inspiration.
- 9:45 A.M.: She gave herself five minutes to jot down some ideas she thought might interest potential clients.
- 9:50 A.M.: She gave herself a forty-minute deadline to complete her first short blog. Time limits are very comforting to an anxious mind. (How much trouble can you get into in forty minutes, after all?)

Now, here's what she didn't do:

- Daydream about wanting to write a blog
- Decide that she needed to stop writing and call her friend back
- Watch three hours of cooking shows on Hulu
- Keep the idea of writing a blog to herself to prevent embarrassment (in case she didn't actually go through with it)

Andrea started. She didn't just *think about* starting a blog. Through the force of her will, she drew a line connecting dream to reality by taking specific actions in the here and now. Simple as that! She didn't wait for lightning bolts of inspiration. She simply got to it, and the Milky Way Moment was already hers.

Now we understand that when Andrea sat at her kitchen table and turned on her laptop, she was already eating her Milky Way. She didn't need to become the most-read blogger in Pasadena to start unwrapping her metaphoric candy bar.

She didn't need to experience the end result. She needed only to start taking action, and Marv went off to read a novel. Endless possibilities arise when we take immediate action.

Andrea is a naturally optimistic person, but that's not to say that midway through the process, she won't have many unwelcome visits from Marv; she will. But it does say that the joy of manifesting a dream doesn't come just at the end.

The fruit of it—the Milky Way Moments—come to you right from the start. But what if Andrea had never taken the precise steps toward writing the blog that led her to her Milky Way Moment? What if she'd just stayed in the anxious mulling-it-over zone?

LAST ODD METAPHOR IN THIS CHAPTER, I PROMISE

Imagine that beside the enormous Milky Way bar is a tiny dried-out blade of grass. That tasteless dried blade of grass represents the amount of pleasure you get from keeping your dream safe inside your head—which, of course, is not much pleasure at all. It's just the measly consolation prize Marv gives you for *not* taking action. As opposed to the Milky Way bar in all its choco-licious splendor, there's no wonderful fragrance from the metaphoric dried blade of grass; you can't get a sugar rush from it. The only thing you can do with it is say, "Won't life be great when I finally get around to [insert your dream here]?" No, it's not a lot of pleasure, certainly not compared with the humongous Milky Way bar.

There actually is one other thing you can do with that worthless dried blade of grass. You can sit around and criticize the people who are having their Milky Way Moments. You can grouse about how much better you'd be if you had a chance to write that song. Or act in that movie. Or start that business. Or write that blog. Now, it would be a lie to say that this kind of passive-aggressiveness yields no delight whatsoever. The truth is that it does . . . sort of. It gives you pleasure perfectly commensurate with a tiny piece of dry grass. Not much, is it?

One reason we so often opt for the grass (i.e., choose not to act on our dreams) is that there's no public shame in not trying. Sure, we might feel bad when we compare ourselves to the Milky Way people but there's not really any loss involved. We never tried, so we never failed.

A MOST PROFOUND
MILKY WAY MOMENT

One of the greatest rewards for taking control of your own thinking (which is exactly what you're doing when you learn to reduce your sense of fear) is that you will instantly become more creative. Understand that by using the term *creative*, I don't mean that you'll suddenly have mastery of any particular skill. What I mean is that the more fearless you can become, the more you will reveal your authentic self. You will act in the here and now, you will have more unfettered access to your previously acquired skill sets, and you will be responsive to what's happening around you. This *freedom to act* is one of the underpinnings of creativity itself; it is, for example, a quality that a jazz pianist must have to be able to improvise well.

One of the most effective methods of eliminating fear is to develop a more profound relationship with the people you love. Science has shown that focusing your creativity on elevating and maintaining those bonds results in the greatest level of overall happiness. Yes, love can make you a more creative person!

Professor and author Barbara L. Fredrickson is the director of the Positive Emotions and Psychophysiology Laboratory, at the University of North Carolina at Chapel Hill. Professor Fredrickson is known for her pioneering research on the long-lasting emotional benefits of human interconnection. She writes about an interesting behavioral quirk called "hedonic adaptation." Simply put, this means that people who win the lottery, for example, find that after a short while, they're no happier than they were before they struck it rich. That's because they've *adapted* to the change.

According to Professor Fredrickson, our relationships with the people we love (unlike our relationship with fame or material gain) are not subject to hedonic adaptation. The positive emotions that accrue from them can last a lifetime. We simply don't adapt to the deep bonds we have with people like we do with a new car or a first-class plane ticket.

Our interactions with loved ones continue to be profound;

they uplift us even with the passage of time. Being generous, expressive, and humble is how we make our relationships strong. When they're strong, we become strong—and better able to make our ideas take shape. Here is a story about how I once told my dad something so important it changed my entire life:

In 1978, I graduated high school, and the "romantic poetry" from Prince's song "Soft and Wet," off his debut album, piqued my imagination. How overt, I wondered, could you possibly get with song lyrics? Inspired by Prince, I wrote several songs, thinking, "It's so damn simple. I can write like this and get famous too!"

Here are the choruses to some of the songs I wrote:

Fireman
I'm your fireman show me where you're burning
I'm your fireman ooh baby I'm coming
I'm your fireman show me where you're burning
And I'll be there to hose you down

Torture Me
Torture me all night long
Love me tough love me strong
I'll be your victim till the break of dawn
Got to move a little faster

Baby Let Me Be Your Cigarette
Baby let me be your cigarette
C'mon and puffa puffa puffa till my tip gets wet
Light me up and baby don't fret
'Cause girl I want to be your cigarette

While I was writing these works of genius—and supposedly having the time of my life—I was in deep emotional pain. My dad discovered a lump in the back of his neck in the autumn of 1978. It took the doctors a week to determine that he had stage IV lymphoma. They figured he had six months, tops. At the time, I was an avid practitioner of Transcendental Meditation; one of its stated goals is that it can help to "flatten" the emotional highs and lows that we normally experience. Because I'd barely reacted when I heard the news, I decided then and there that something that could make me this flat and nonresponsive to what should have been devastating couldn't be good; I vowed to quit TM that very night.

I understood later that it wasn't the TM that had flattened me, but my own propensity to go inside myself, to stay as far away from my feelings as possible. It was as if I'd been playing a sort of double role. On one hand I remained hypersensitive and very connected to the grief I was experiencing. On the other, I was divorced from my emotions and totally shut down. Years later, toward the end of my dad's life, everything came crashing in as the two halves collided.

It was 1983 and I was in Amery, Wisconsin. Our band had finished up its last set at a bar called the Country Dam. It was late and the crowd was so drunk that they were falling over one another, screaming for one more chorus of "Fireman." At four in the morning I pulled up to my parents' house behind my dad's white '83 Chrysler LeBaron; he'd gone all the way to Mankato with my mother to buy this thing. Tired as I was, I couldn't stop looking at this car, wondering how I'd feel about it when he died. It was Father's Day, after all, and my mom had planned a big brunch for him in just a few hours. Cousins, aunts, and uncles—everybody wanted to be there and cheer him up. My mom had asked me to write something funny, some kind of cute ditty to lighten the mood. Even though my dad had outlived the doctor's dire predictions by four years, we knew that the cancer had progressed to the point where this was very likely his last Father's Day.

I was still pretty wound up from the performance the night before and since the sun was coming up anyway, I couldn't see any reason to try and sleep. I picked up a guitar. It was an old nylon-string that hardly played in tune. I started picking through some chords in a half trance and began singing softly to myself, just thinking about that LeBaron and how my dad really liked it. The words came fast and the melody started to take on a shape. Each new line generated more melody and the melody inspired more words.

> *When no one is forgotten and nothing goes to waste, when sadness turns to laughter, when anger is defaced . . .*
> *. . . you'll start to know the way I feel about you.*

I knew from experience that when a song comes to you like that, it's best to get out of your own way, to be as detached as possible, and yet I couldn't help feeling excited that this was a song for my dad. I thought, "At least now I won't be the only fool at the brunch without a Father's Day present."

> *And if I could, I'd run out into the world and tell every boy and girl, to love before love takes itself away . . . just like I'm loving you this Father's Day.*

I made a quick recording of the song and I was so tired and so emotional that I started crying in the last chorus. I didn't want to let everyone hear me blubbering on tape, so I reached over to erase it and sing it again, but at the last second I decided to leave it as was, tears and all. Around ten o'clock that morning I came upstairs with the cassette. By then the brunch was in full swing: The lox and the smoked whitefish had been taken out of the refrigerator and arranged on separate platters. The scrambled eggs and onions were warming on the stove. The cinnamon rolls and the pitchers of Minute Maid were on the table and the brunch-goers were trying their best to slap on their happiest faces. When I popped the cassette into the stereo, I swear, it took no more than ten seconds for everyone to break down in tears and exit the room.

It was just my dad and me now, both of us staring out the big picture window of our den, listening as the song played. As it ended, we held each other and cried. Whatever facade of normalcy we'd been putting up over the past several months washed away in the emotion of that song. I'd wanted to say so many things to him, and for so long. Somehow the song expressed everything so well. From that morning on, my dad carried the cassette around with him in his breast pocket. He died a few months later, on Thanksgiving night. We got a call from the hospital as we were sitting at the table; the turkey was never carved. As tragic and sad as his death was, I've never felt that I was remiss in expressing how I felt.

Putting my emotions on display in that song was hard. Nonetheless, I felt close enough to my dad to keep the recording intact and play it for everyone. As Professor Fredrickson explains, in contrast to our material possessions, the joy we derive from our most loving relationships does not diminish over time. In terms of creativity, this suggests to me that those deep relationships can gird us to withstand our innate fear of failure. Knowing that we have a rock-solid support system gives us the strength to ignore our self-critical voices and to reclaim a childlike relationship with the world. That support was my dad's priceless gift to me.

Note: A year after my dad died, the song I'd written for him became the title track to a record called *This Father's Day*. It was that song and that album—not "Fireman" or "Torture Me"—that eventually got me my first major-label recording deal, with Island Records, in 1985. Imagine that!

Now, in this next Brain Bottle Opener, I'm going to give you an opportunity to do something very similar to what I did when I wrote that song for my dad, something that will help bring you the kind of joy that is definitely not subject to hedonic adaptation.

Me and my dad, 1979

Brain Bottle Opener 5: Smartphone Letter

Hardly a day goes by without hearing that the iPhone (and all the other smartphones in the world) is destroying our humanity, our ability to communicate, to bond with others, and even to think. I beg to differ. I may be a lone voice out there, but I offer this: The smartphone is the most connective and most humanizing device ever created. Like every piece of technology, from the knife to the violin, the way we use it determines whether it delivers pleasure or pain.

I want you to take **three minutes** to write a text or an e-mail on your smartphone to someone you love, someone who's been a mentor, a guide, a positive force in your life. Do it right now. Tell that person everything you'd want them to know, as if his or her survival into the next day were an uncertainty. (And whose isn't?)

Now *send* it!

That's right: Take your index finger and hit Send.

Writing the Smartphone Letter and hitting Send are real actions, of course, but they are also powerful metaphors. You took a nascent idea (your love for the person you wrote to) and brought it through "the pinhole," as my filmmaker friend Jim Hershleder likes to say.

In that special moment while you were writing, your thoughts became transmuted into reality. They became a written depiction of your feelings and took on a new, more genuine dimension. By hitting Send you drew that idea one step further into reality through the act of sharing.

I recently received an e-mail from a participant in one of my Big Muse workshops, Brad G., a successful Chicago businessman, in which he described how this particular BBO changed his life. Brad told me that he and his eighty-eight-year-old father always had a somewhat distant relationship, that he'd never once heard his father say, "I'm proud of you" or "I love you." Then he went on to tell me that he sent his father a text during one of my seminars that said simply:

> Dad, I don't think I've ever told you this, but I really love you.

Within minutes he received a text message from each of his sisters.

> OMG, Brad, are you going down in a plane crash?

> Brad, are you okay, did you just get a terminal diagnosis?

Then came the response that Brad had been waiting all his life to hear:

> Brad, I love you too, and I've always been so proud of you. I'm so sorry this has always been so difficult for me to say.

The postscript to this story is that since the Smartphone Letter Brad sent to his dad, his whole family has been communicating on a deeper level, with more frequent calls and more exchanges of real affection.

REAL-WORLD APPLICATIONS

In many ways this BBO is like the Swiss Army knife of Brain Bottle Openers. It is a powerful, all-purpose technique for reducing anxiety. Let's say, for example, that you've been tasked with writing a long and complicated legal brief. The weight of the effort is looming over you. The due date is causing you tremendous anxiety and you feel like you'd do anything to stave it off. Know that this is a perfect time for the Smartphone Letter. There is a fear-reducing aspect to this BBO that often makes mountains shrink immediately into molehills.

Now, you may be saying, "How can I write something 'heartfelt' on command? How can doing something for the sake of an exercise, particularly one that's designed to help me with a mundane business task, ever be real—or moral, for that matter?" The magic of this BBO is that despite what you're thinking before you commence writing to a loved one, when you actually start the Smartphone Letter, you will be doing it from a place of truth. You will go from an intellectual process directly to an emotional one, and the fact that you're moving from one to the other in seconds makes no difference at all. This is all about *doing*. Your mere thoughts about how it won't work are just that—thoughts. Once you begin to act—in this case to write—everything changes. Try it and you'll see.

CHAPTER 6

KID-THINKING AND KARATE KICKS

HOW THINKING LIKE A CHILD CAN GIVE US GROWN-UP INSIGHTS

D. W. Winnicott, the famed English pediatrician and psychoanalyst, wrote extensively on the subject of play. Here's one of the ways he describes it: "Without hallucinating, the child puts out a sample of dream potential and lives with this sample in a chosen setting of fragments from external reality."

In other words, the child engaged in play is taking material from his or her inner reality, or dream world, and placing it into external reality—what we might call the real world. Play then becomes the intersection of dream and reality. I call that potent, unfettered, creative mind-set that happens when we're deep inside the Milky Way Moment "Kid-Thinking." It's how we think and act when we fully immerse ourselves in joyous doing. We are mingling dreams with reality when we are at play. Very young children don't think about the consequences of playing; they just play. They're not afraid of how they'll look or how they'll be perceived. That comes later.

It's an interesting evolutionary quirk that even though we are hardwired to abhor failure, we rarely get important information from our successes. It's the times we've come up short of our expectations that give us what is arguably our most important life lesson: *Failure won't kill us.* Trusting this on a visceral level allows us to create the way we did when we were kids. For some, it might feel like a regression to revert to the way they created when they were children. This wasn't the case for world-renowned artist Pablo Picasso. He was once quoted as saying, "When I was a child, I painted like a master and now, as a man, I strive to paint like a child."

MY WIFE AND I studied karate for nearly ten years, and even though we eventually got our black belts from the legendary sensei Hidetaka Nishiyama, I always knew I'd never gotten to a level where I could use karate to truly defend myself. This isn't uncommon. Karate is an incredibly difficult skill to use, let alone master. It's my belief that for every three hundred practitioners, only one of them is actually doing karate well. That is to say, these rare people (the one out of three hundred) can perceive exactly when an opponent is even thinking of throwing a punch or delivering a kick. Then, using that special sense they've developed over years of training, they know within milliseconds which offensive or defensive techniques to apply.

One of the (many) reasons I was never the one out of three hundred is simple: I was always afraid of getting hit. You might be thinking that karate, at least on some level, is all about hitting and getting hit, but as a professional guitarist, I was understandably overprotective of my hands; as a result, my timing was always slightly off. I was always reacting too slowly, hesitating for fear that I might break a finger or two.

The few people I knew who actually were karate experts didn't share my aversion to getting hit. In fact, they'd been hit hundreds of times, and because of this, they knew that while unpleasant, it just wasn't a big deal. They knew that the small "failure" of getting kicked in the ribs, breaking a pinkie, or taking a smack to the jaw wasn't a failure at all; it was an opportunity to sharpen a skill. Without the fear of failure impeding them, they were ultimately almost always able to strike offensively or block defensively with success.

Kid-Thinking is wonderful, but it's a state of mind that is not always accessible. What is accessible is the ability to simply observe how our fears might be preventing our Kid-Thinking from taking place. Are you afraid of getting hit? And if so, what does "getting hit" feel like to you? Is the pain you fear greater in theory than in fact?

Now of course there are some things that you really should fear: falling out of an airplane with no parachute, being chased by a hungry cheetah, or speaking in front of hundreds of people with absolutely nothing to say. But most of our fears are not really fears at all. They're harmless anxieties. We often get them mixed up. The book *Synopsis of Psychiatry* has been a best-selling psychology text since 1972. Authors Harold Kaplan and Benjamin Sadock write: "Anxiety is a diffuse, unpleasant, vague sense of apprehension, and fear is an emotional response to a known or definite threat."

So, if you're at the zoo and you happen to fall into the frigid water of the polar bear exhibit, be very afraid—that's real fear you're experiencing. Those cute white bears can swat your head off with a flick of a paw, I'm told. But if you're having trouble sleeping at night because random unsettling thoughts keep popping up in your mind, know that you're experiencing Kaplan and Sadock's textbook description of anxiety. Anxiety can often be countered by taking specific problem-solving actions. As for falling into the polar bear exhibit . . . Let's just say your problem-solving skills better be really good.

The following story is from a master Kid-Thinker who managed to get down to business in spite of his anxieties. Let's see what we can learn from him.

PEPPERCORNS, PASSION, AND THE PURSUIT OF DOUBLE DREAMS

In 1996, when entrepreneur Scott Eirinberg's wife was newly pregnant with their first child, he began looking around for children's furniture. Scott was working in advertising at the time and he immediately saw that there were just two types of children's furniture out there: junky, gaudy stuff at the low end, crap you'd never want in your home if you could avoid it; and fussy, superexpensive stuff at the high end. Scott saw a need for something in the middle, children's furniture that was fun, hip, and high quality, and that also didn't cost a fortune. After he considered all this, a lightbulb in his Kid-Thinking brain flashed on. With very little money and even less experience as a retailer, Scott and a partner started what would eventually become a hugely successful children's furnishings company, the Land of Nod.

In launching the business, Scott started by doing the things he wanted to do, things he really loved, such as product design and creative marketing. When we sat down to speak, he still seemed amazed that he'd essentially created a national brand from a blank sheet of paper. It had all taken place one afternoon when Scott just happened to say to his wife, Karla, "How come there isn't a Crate and Barrel for kids' rooms?" Scott was intrigued by his own question. He toyed with it a little and made it more of a proactive statement: *We want to be the Crate and Barrel of kids' rooms.*

I listened as Scott told me how he'd just sat for a while and pondered the idea. The more he thought, the more he became engaged by the possibilities it contained. He couldn't have known how fortuitous his next action would be, but like so many of the things we've been exploring in this book, it was a tiny step but one that was so significant. He sat down and typed out that short statement, "We want to be the Crate and Barrel of kids' rooms," printed it on an old-school dot matrix printer, and hung it on the wall in his office. All Scott had at the time was that one idea, an idea so concise that it boiled down to one sentence. I asked him how writing it had changed things for him. "I think having that vision about where we wanted to go was key," he said. "Even though we had no idea whatsoever how to get there, we had our destination."

I personally find Scott's Crate and Barrel comparison fascinating. It's such a great crystallization of his idea, and he put it in terms that anyone can understand. It's as if Scott could visualize his entire business through the lens of that one focused sentence. I'd go so far as to say that if he hadn't actually written it down, there's a good chance the idea might have just floated away.

I asked Scott to tell me about his doubts; I assumed he had some big ones. As he spoke he got more and more animated. "At first," he said, "I was so worried—could we really make this business work, could we really make a living doing this? Then it got worse. It was like, 'Wow, Scott, this is a *really* stupid idea! Are you a total idiot? You left a job where you were making sixty-five thousand a year, now you're not drawing a salary, your wife is pregnant, and you could lose your house and your life savings!'"

His wife helped a lot during those tidal waves of negativity. "Karla was my rock," he said. "She'd calm me down. She'd say, 'No, it's a good idea. We've been here before. Come on, you can do this.' She'd pick me up. Eventually I would just shrug it off and we'd keep moving."

Finding the right person to bolster your confidence is a central component in bringing your dream into reality; we'll discuss this more in Chapter 16. I do, however, want to point out the universality of this experience of doubt. It's not that people who are able to make their goals manifest have some superhuman strength or unlimited resources, or that their objectives are so profound. The sense that an idea may be so stupid it's going to "do you in" is ubiquitous and unavoidable. But what Scott did that enabled his idea to continue to expand was the opposite of isolating himself and letting his fear take control (always a bad idea). He sought the support and guidance of someone he trusted—in this case, his wife—

and in doing so, he enlisted an ally who kept him from drowning in the waters of pessimism. It's very difficult to save yourself when you're slipping under the waves.

Almost two decades later, after building the Land of Nod into a thriving and innovative company, things started to change. For Scott, working at the company he had helped to create, the company that was once a source of deep engagement and personal expression, slowly become drudgery. As he moved from the creative work he was passionate about, such as product development and marketing, to managing people, he felt the playfulness leech out of the whole experience.

Eventually Scott gave notice to his board. Then, after he took nearly three years off to travel, enjoy his family, and consider his next move, Scott's Kid-Thinking kicked in once again. Rather unexpectedly and somewhat reluctantly (as he put it), Scott began the journey of starting yet another company from scratch: a spice company, another thing he claimed to know nothing about, which he eventually called the Reluctant Trading Experiment.

During his time at the Land of Nod, Scott had purchased many of his textiles in India through a guy named Divakar. It was Divakar who first called Scott about an amazing Tellicherry black peppercorn he'd discovered. Divakar's dream was for Scott to distribute it in the United States. Unfortunately for Divakar, Scott wasn't biting. Scott had no knowledge or interest in anything to do with food. But Divakar was persistent and he sent Scott a sample. One taste later, Scott was hooked. Like most people, he'd always thought pepper was pepper, but this was different. It was so compelling, in fact, that Scott started thinking seriously about ways to create a business around it.

I was most interested in how this particular idea stuck with him. How did it not just slip away into the ether? Scott told me that the whole business model and the name itself were just crazy enough and interesting enough for him to want to turn it into a brand. "The name, the Reluctant Trading Experiment," he said with a sly smile, "came about because I was so reluctant, after all. But the more I thought about it, the more I was convinced I should start selling this unbelievably good pepper under my own brand name. I think you have to be honest with yourself. I didn't try to convince myself it was the best pepper in the world just because I tasted it once and thought it was great. I went out and found a great chef to tell me what he thought of it and I didn't pay him to get his opinion. Then I went out and did a blind taste test that confirmed my opinion."

It wasn't that Scott possessed some special knowledge. It wasn't that he had incredible self-discipline either. It was just his passion for the taste of that Tellicherry pepper that compelled him to:

- create a name for his spice company;
- create a website;
- create a blog;
- begin selling to consumers; and
- develop the emotional strength to withstand the inevitable criticism (from without and within).

He did all these very specific things in the present—the here and now. This dream of his was an outgrowth of his Kid-Thinking and his love of telling true stories. As he put it, it was just a way for him to be authentic.

Brain Bottle Opener 6: From Chaos to Kid-Thinking

Anthony McCaffrey, a cognitive psychology researcher at the University of Massachusetts, Amherst, has done extensive research on the idea of functional fixedness and the effects it has on strengthening our ability to think more creatively. Functional fixedness is something we'll revisit in this book because it's so relevant to understanding ways to improve our problem-solving skills. It works like this:

When someone sees an object—a ceramic cup, for example—he or she will typically think of it as what it is. In this case, it's something to drink from. That would be its "fixed" function. But what if we were tasked with quickly seeing five other things it could be used for? We would then be moving away from functional fixedness and toward Kid-Thinking. I've just given myself two minutes to see the cup as:

A hat for a doll
A hoop for a mini-basketball game
A cutting tool (if you broke the cup into shards)
A high-pitched percussion instrument (if you tap it with a pen)
A paperweight
A cup for a shell game
A circle tracer
A small planter

You can try it with anything you see around you. Give yourself **two minutes** and create your own list.

Now in that same vein, I want you to take a pencil and make a scribble on a piece of paper. Just let your hand go free and scribble out anything. Then, much like you might see shapes and images in a cloud formation, use the pencil to "connect the dots" and highlight what you see. They could be faces or animals—whatever comes to mind. Do three of these and give yourself no more than **two minutes** for each one.

When you do these drawings quickly, without thinking too much or worrying about the "art" of it, they're a great brain stimulator. The trick is not to think but to react. Too much analysis doesn't help this exercise. If you go with your first impressions and aren't afraid that you won't uncover anything hiding in the scribbles, you'll find that it's a lot of fun. (Don't be afraid to turn the paper to get different angles—anything to change your perspective is fair game!)

Also, you'll find that once you see the face or the shape, you'll never be able to view the "randomness" of the original scribble again. Here are a few of mine:

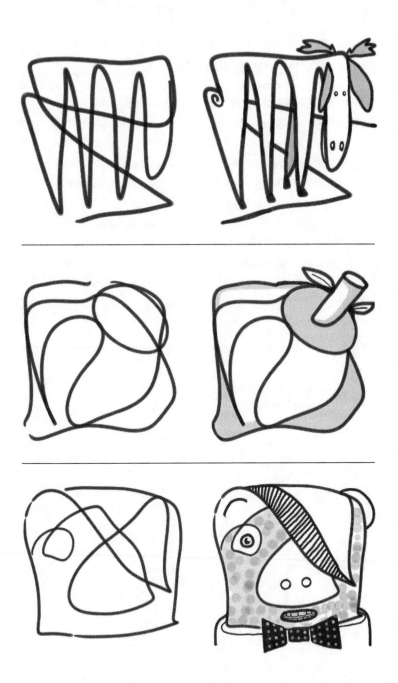

REAL-WORLD APPLICATIONS

Aside from the fact that From Chaos to Kid-Thinking is a really fun BBO, it's also a powerful tool to jump-start innovative thinking. Let's say you're on a marketing team and you need to come up with names for a new food product. Doing this BBO before or at your company's next ideation session would be a great way to give your mind access to wild new ideas, weird thoughts, and associations that seem to come from a radically unfamiliar place. Get used to the notion that many of these radically unfamiliar ideas are not going to be useful in the traditional sense. The larger point is that if you allow your mind to travel to unaccustomed places, the chances that you'll find something wonderful increase tremendously.

CHAPTER 7

RECOGNIZING STUCK-THINKING

HOW RETHINKING CREATIVITY CAN FREE OUR MINDS

Why is it that we seem to have a societal tendency to label people as either "creative" or "not creative"? The misunderstandings that result from such judgments might, for example, lead us to assume that a performance artist with nipple rings is the natural heir to all things innovative, while the white-bread actuary has little capacity for abstract thought. But in reality, creativity is more akin to something like gravity—a natural force and condition that is available to everyone, not just a select few. Remember, creativity should not be mistaken for mastery; they're two very different things.

Creativity is a state of being; mastery is excellence in a set of specific skills.

Anthony McCaffrey, whom I mentioned in the preceding chapter, gives scientific credence to the idea that creativity can indeed be learned just like reading, math, or athletic skills. In one of his better-known experiments, he looked at more than one hundred important modern and one thousand historical inventions, specifically to find out how successful inventors solved problems. What he discovered became the basis for his theory about functional fixedness, a common mental obstacle. Here's an example of what he's talking about:

Imagine two people tramping through the woods. Person A finds burrs stuck to his sweater and thinks, "Crap, all these burrs are ruining my new sweater." But person B, who is less functionally fixed, thinks, "Hmm, two things lightly fastened together . . ." and then he invents Velcro. Person A has a perspective that's creatively limited because he focuses only on an object's typical function; a burr is always a burr and nothing else. Person B has a way of seeing things for what they could be.

By eliminating functional fixedness, or Stuck-Thinking, as I like to call it, we can open up to our creative potential. A first step in getting past being a Stuck-Thinker is to unlearn some commonly held notions about what constitutes creativity and who and what should be considered creative in the first place. Our blind faith in stereotypes of all kinds has the profoundly negative effect of dampening our creative capacities. (It also confirms that we've remained functionally fixed.)

First, Unlearn This! These Are Our Creative Types:

- Painters
- Poets
- Dancers
- Musicians
- Filmmakers
- Actors
- Authors
- Sculptors
- Inventors
- Designers

Next, Unlearn This! These Are Our Noncreative Types:

- Insurance salesmen
- Mortgage brokers
- Housekeepers
- Mail carriers
- Actuaries
- Accountants
- Managers
- Farmers
- Attorneys
- Mechanics

These assumptive categories are popular, but like many generalizations that gain traction, they're also ridiculous and misleading. Take Joe Fischer, for example. He's a certified financial planner working for a well-known private-wealth firm in New York City.

He's actually a very creative person, but because his father told him he wasn't, he spent most of his life thinking otherwise. In fact, Joe's creativity shines in his marketing strategies to attract new customers. It's apparent in the way he bonds with his longtime clients, and it manifests itself most notably in the way he interacts with his family. He's always surprising them in funny ways, like the time he hid a diamond ring he bought for his wife's birthday at the bottom of a bucket of Kentucky Fried Chicken—or the time he brought home a baby sulcata tortoise (the world's third-largest species of tortoise) when his daughter was studying Darwinism in eleventh grade.

On the other hand, people like me, who've hung the proverbial artist shingle over their door, may in practice be in very uncreative phases of their lives, working too hard toward the goal of becoming better known rather than working innovatively on the details of a piece of music or a painting. In my own life, I've found that my oft-repeated pattern is to have some sort of intense breakthrough every few months (okay, every few years) that causes me to momentarily look at music and songwriting with new eyes. I become a Kid-Thinker again, alive to the experience of writing. Then, because it's such an exquisite sensation to work with these new ideas, I can't help but repeat myself again and again. I don't stop until I catch myself thinking, "Hey, wait a minute, you're not creating a damn thing; you're just popping out copies again." That I'm making music, an ostensibly creative endeavor, simply hides the fact that I'm often on autopilot and merely making clones of my original creative impetus.

*   *   *

JUST AS A person's character isn't defined by his or her race, religion, economic status, or gender, people's creative capacities can never be determined by their job titles. Creativity can exist in every arena of human endeavor, not just the ones that sound creative.

Whether something positive actually results from our behavior is an ideal yardstick for measuring what's truly creative and what's not. Of course, that yardstick is the most individual thing in the world; only we can accurately determine what those positive results are. One hint, though: A creative endeavor almost always makes something constructive happen, fostering some kind of positive growth. When we apply ourselves wholeheartedly to the things we love, it's as if we imbue them with new life.

As we invest our time, money, or other resources in something or someone, our love for that thing invariably grows. Our joy and our life's rewards don't come from entertainment and distractions. They come exclusively from our intense, passionate interaction with the things and people we love, the ideas and people we wholly give our minds and creativity to. There is no other known pathway to joy. When we say someone is passionate about something, it's typically said as the highest praise. The most skilled artists, athletes, entrepreneurs, and poets are all thought to be passionate, each willing to give his or her all.

I find it interesting that the etymological root of the word *passion* is from the late Latin *passionem* (normative *passio*), which means "suffering, misery, or woe." Look, I don't know anyone who wants suffering, misery, or woe, and unless you're a masochist (and who's judging?) you probably don't want suffering either. But our culture has grown so enamored with joy's younger cousin, fun, that we've forgotten just how much hard work it often takes to create real lasting joy.

THE FUN CONUNDRUM
AND THE PASSION PARADOX

We are constantly being sold the idea that we can derive joy from amusement, and so we are fed endless videos, infinite hours of recorded music, electronic games so real they begin to supplant reality, pornography that's anonymous and free at the click of a mouse, movies on demand . . . relentless buzzing, lights flashing, words projected, products proffered, senses overloaded . . . all to hypnotize us into buying more amusements that lure us into the notion that we're having fun, and worst of all, that fun is joy. Fun isn't joy. Compared to *true* joy, fun is thin, transient, fleeting, momentary, replaceable, and self-serving. Joy is broad, all-encompassing, deep, lasting, eternal, irreplaceable, generous, and often very costly in one sense or another. Hey, I've got no beef with fun; it's wonderful and necessary. But there's a problem when we as a society begin to think of fun and joy as synonymous.

Here's the challenge: Knowing that our joy is bound up in our dedication to the people and things we truly love and that without that dedication we can have no joy, we need to be able to endure the burden that necessarily goes along with that dedication, both as individuals and as a society.

That's the nature and the cost of joy. It boils down to this: Can we stave off the smaller momentary gain for a larger subsequent one?

We all admire people who have that kind of endurance. A great deal of what we're seeing when we're watching NBA star LeBron James, for example, is the personification of his dedication to basketball. He becomes the human exemplar of endurance. It's the same when we're listening to the cellist Yo-Yo Ma or the late, great gospel singer Mahalia Jackson or looking at sculpture by Michelangelo. We are moved, of course, by the grace and art we're witnessing, but we're also moved by the enormity of these people's dedication, by their ability to endure. Suffering, misery, and woe don't sound like a lot of fun, and perhaps they're terms that are too strong. But the larger point is that our utter commitment to our goals is the shortest path to joy, perhaps the only path to real joy.

One more simple way to determine if you're acting creatively is to see whether possibilities for positive change have contracted or expanded. In other words, are you seeing a situation or tackling a challenge from the perspective of a Kid-Thinker or a Stuck-Thinker?

A Kid-Thinker, as we've learned, acts in the moment; she's not swayed by outside forces or inner turbulence. She's free of negative emotions and able to look at things differently. A Stuck-Thinker is just the opposite. He's trapped in the status quo, and because he's often swayed by his emotions, he can barely imagine how a thing or situation can ever be different from how it appears.

Being an observer requires being in the moment. Being in the moment is our state of mind when we are at our creative best. Getting yourself into that mental state can be learned, and consistently practicing what you've learned so far in this book is a good way of regaining what many of us lost as we moved from childhood to adolescence and into adulthood.

YOU CAN START your practice of staying a Kid-Thinker with fairly easy exercises utilizing things you find around you every day. For example, when someone butts in line ahead of you at the 7-Eleven, try not to lose your cool. But be forewarned, you'll have just a second or two to choose whether you want to become upset or not. Your window of volition will be there, but it's very small. The better you get at maintaining your observer status—that is, watching yourself before you get carried off by your emotions—the more you will be able to (1) remain in control of your decision-making faculties, (2) stay in the present, and (3) increase your capacity for empathic thinking.

AN ANCIENT TEXT called *Ethics of the Fathers* describes four distinct personality types:

1. Slow to anger, quick to pacify
2. Quick to anger, quick to pacify
3. Slow to anger, slow to pacify
4. Quick to anger, slow to pacify

Can you see yourself in any of these? The best of the bunch is number one, of course. This person hardly ever gets angry and when he does, he's easy to cheer up.

At the bottom of the list is the least desirable personality type: easily annoyed and very difficult to assuage. I'm a number three. It takes a lot to make me angry. I pride myself on the fact that I only get steamin' mad about once every five or six years. The bad part is that when I do get angry, I go a bit nuts.

THE NONREFUNDABLE CHEESE INCIDENT

I'm slightly embarrassed to share this next story with you, because it illustrates one of the aforementioned "once every five or six years" episodes in which I fail so miserably at not losing my cool but here goes:

One morning I drove to my favorite market and purchased two bags of cheese for some homemade pizza I was planning to make. I opened the first bag and there was a big wad of green mold at the top. The second bag didn't have any visible mold but it smelled of decaying muskrat. "No big deal," I thought to myself; the pizza could wait, and I decided to take the bags of rotten cheese back to the store in the morning. I got there early and the guy at the register told me he couldn't do an exchange because I didn't have my receipt. My pulse rate went up slightly.

"Well, can you please get the manager? Because I spend quite a bit at this store and it doesn't make sense that you can't do an exchange," I said.

The refrigerated foods guy came to the register and said the same thing. "No receipt, no exchange." My pulse rate spiked a bit more.

"Guys," I said. "I understand that you're obviously parroting the owner's general rule but in this case intelligence dictates that you abandon dogmatic principle for a broader view. Namely, that you'll be in better stead with the store owner, the guy who writes your checks, if you exchange the rotten cheese than you will be if you lose my hundreds, if not thousands of dollars of business over this matter."

Blank looks all around. Then the owner walked in, and I launched into my explanation of the problem with renewed vigor.

He looked at me and said, "Do you have a receipt?"

Now there was smoke—not a lot, but definitely some smoke—starting to leak out of my ears.

"You gotta be kidding! All I want to do is exchange these moldy bags of cheese. I'm not trying to rip you off; I just want two new bags of cheese!"

The store owner was remarkably calm and it pissed me off all the more. "That's our policy," he said. "How do I know where you bought this cheese and how you stored it? Maybe you left it outside for a week."

"Oh my god!" I shouted. "You've got to be insane. Why on earth would I be driving around town with two bags of moldering cheese? How could I possibly profit from a scam like this? Do you seriously think I'm the guy making millions by doing exchanges on cheese, two bags at a time?"

The more enraged I became, the calmer the store owner seemed to get. "I'm not calling you a liar," he kept saying, and of course, that just made me crazier. Finally he said, "If your wife comes in and buys as much as you say she does, than she can come find me and if I see that her cart is full, I'll exchange one of the bags of cheese."

I slammed the two bags I'd been holding on the counter. "You're a total dick!" I shouted and headed out to my car.

Back home, still enraged, I called Visa to see exactly how much we actually spent at this store. It was a lot. Close to five grand a year. Then I began writing a letter to make this loser see just what a total moron he was, and how he'd sacrificed a five-thousand-dollar customer relationship for two bags of rotten cheese. Fortunately, I had the presence of mind to forward the letter to my son Isaac. He told me that it was great to be able to vent, but that under no circumstances should I send the letter.

"Dad, you sound like a raving lunatic," he said. (Leave it to my kid to bring me back to Kid-Thinking.)

It's true, I did. And what was worse, I really liked shopping at that store. Who was the loser now? Slow to anger, slow to pacify, indeed. And here's the issue, looking back: Is that condition of mine, *slow to pacify*, an indelible part of who I am, of how I must behave? I'd truly like to be slow to anger and quick to pacify. And maybe you would too. To do so I'd have to become empathetic enough to see the store owner's point of view. Here's what I came up with:

- Though I totally disagree with his policy and his intransigent stance, I must admit that I don't know a thing about running a store.
- The store owner told me that he's got people trying to exchange things all day long. Maybe he was telling the truth and maybe those exchanges cut into his profits. As I said, I didn't know anything about his overhead or what he pays his employees or his profit margins.
- Perhaps getting insane in the middle of his store was not only bad for his business, but painted me as . . . well, an insane person.
- Perhaps if I'd taken him aside and explained my situation in private, it would have been easier for him to make an exception to his exchange policy.
- It's possible there were language and cultural considerations that I hadn't thought about . . . especially as the smoke poured out of my ears.
- Finally, and most important, why should this guy make an exception for me anyway?

And so, continuing with my experiment, I decided to do what had previously been unthinkable: I called the store owner and apologized. I didn't cast any blame on him, or on myself, for that matter. I simply reiterated the list I'd made. Here's what he said: "You have no idea how happy this makes me. No one understands the kinds of pressure I'm under with people running into my store every minute to exchange things they didn't even buy here. I would have gladly exchanged your cheese but it wouldn't have been possible to do so in public. Please," he said, "come back to my store, I'll exchange the cheese, we'll sit and have tea and some cake."

Having the ability to see our lives objectively, as though from a great height, is always an advantage. Try this following Brain Bottle Opener and see if it doesn't help open up your Stuck-Thinking.

Brain Bottle Opener 7: The Walk-Away

This is yet another take on reducing functional fixedness, and I think you'll have a lot of fun with it. It's a slightly strange idea, but it's had a remarkable effect on helping me and others become more of a Kid-Thinker.

Single out any random object you see in front of you. Let's use a kitchen table for our example. First see the table for what it is (most likely wood). Then take a metaphoric step back and the wood becomes: a tree, then a seed, then two hands planting the seed, then the face of a young boy who's planting the seed, then the house where the boy lives, the bed he sleeps in, the moonlight streaming in from his window, and the heat of the sun that makes the moon shine. . . . Continue uninterrupted in this fashion for about **two minutes**, until the table you started out with becomes something completely unrecognizable.

The fun part of this experiment is seeing how the dissimilarity between a kitchen table and moonlight, for example—two things that usually have nothing in common—melts away once you consider all the in-between steps.

REAL-WORLD APPLICATIONS

If you were tasked with finding new ways to solve a problem, whether scientific or social, using the Walk-Away BBO would help train your mind to discover patterns and relationships that are not readily apparent.

Scotch tape, one of the 3M Company's most famous products, came about when a young researcher named Richard Drew was exploring ways a "flawed" adhesive could be used. Drew eventually found that if he applied the adhesive, with its less-than-ideal stickiness, to the company's newly invented cellophane tape, it would be perfect for creating the two-tone paint jobs that were in style on cars in the 1930s. This new kind of tape would adhere to the car's surface, but it was not so sticky that it would damage the paint when it was removed.

Note of interest: The use of the term *Scotch* in the name was a pejorative meaning "stingy" in the 1920s and 1930s. One of the body shop painters who first used the tape became frustrated with its lack of adhesive material. He was said to have shouted, "Take this tape back to those Scotch bosses of yours and tell them to put more adhesive on it!" The name was soon applied to the entire line of 3M tapes.

PART TWO REVIEW

IN THIS MOST recent part:

- You moved directly into the Milky Way Moment by writing a letter on your smartphone to someone you love, and you shared that love. By doing so, you created a deeper bond and a greater sense of trust. Since one of our primal fears is abandonment, this BBO creates a climate in which we feel more connected and consequently less threatened. The diminution in threat naturally leaves us open to creativity. Now from within the Milky Way Moment you're ready to move on to all sorts of creative ways of looking at things.

- You used Kid-Thinking to make order out of chaos by searching for recognizable images in the midst of random scribbles. This is one of the most powerful methods of moving instantly away from Stuck-Thinking.

- Finally, by doing the Walk-Away BBO you went one step further. You took recognized objects and ideas and expanded them beyond their typical meanings. This allows you to see possibilities where you thought there were none. The Walk-Away is another tremendous boost to your Kid-Thinking.

If you're intimidated by some pending important creative project, shining a light on your Elephant Ropes can be a significant help. Kid-Thinking can help you reduce your fears. But knowing there's a Milky Way Moment out there to inspire you doesn't in itself make you more able to achieve your dreams. You need a plan—a process.

In this next part we'll focus on the actual nuts and bolts of unleashing your Big Muse and moving your dream out into the real world.

PART THREE

THE PROCESS

The secret of getting ahead is getting started. The secret of getting started is breaking your complex, overwhelming tasks into small, manageable tasks, and then starting on that first one.

-Mark Twain

CHAPTER 8

BE PRESENT

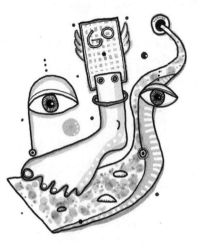

FINDING YOUR NEXT STEP

We may intend to be present and take action immediately on our goals, but we often run into distractions, temptations, and interruptions. Is there any way to avoid this? If we quickly undertake just one small part of a daunting project, we will have less interference from our negative emotions and we'll be able to experience the Milky Way Moment. Once we're there, the distractions that called out to us as we sat obsessing over them will seem far less inviting. The Milky Way Moment will then afford us the opportunity to be in something I call the HourGlass.

I'll bet you've found yourself in the HourGlass at some point. It's when you're so engaged in whatever it is you're doing that time loses its dimensions. You could be painting. You could be writing a legal brief. You could be fly-fishing in Montana or playing Ping-Pong with your niece. In the HourGlass, time suddenly has no relevance. It's a wonderful sensation, but forcing it to happen and actually trying to achieve it is impossible. What is helpful in bringing on the HourGlass is diving into the details and finding the joy in the sensations, the emotions, and even the challenges your creative process engenders.

It's a little-known fact, but in author/artist Mihaly Csikszentmihalyi's earliest research on the creative process, he discovered the true meaning of the phrase "starving artist" while studying young painters. Most of us associate the term with destitute but zealous art students. Interestingly, it has nothing to do with their socioeconomic status at all. The term derives from the idea that these passionate painters are so wrapped up in their work—so fully present and working within the HourGlass—that they never get up to eat. Csikszentmihalyi labeled this "flow." It's impossible to be in the HourGlass if you're a Stuck-Thinker.

Aside from some minor variations, Stuck-Thinkers come in two basic styles: Idea Bunnies and Blocked-Heads. Idea Bunnies are people who are overwhelmed with too many good choices. They can't decide what to devote their energies to and instead they wind up not doing much of anything. The Blocked-Head is a person who's so trapped by fear that she's unable to even imagine what she wants to accomplish with her time on earth. Though Idea Bunnies and Blocked-Heads would seem like exact opposites, they actually represent two sides of the same coin.

I often hear people say that they don't know what they want to do next in life. I don't believe them. I believe they've become Stuck-Thinkers and that they use *not knowing* as a way of staying safe from the pain of failure. Think about it: Who really doesn't know what they want? Peach ice cream or mint chip, wild sex or a walk around the lake? Our will naturally pulls us toward the things we desire and away from the things we loathe. It's native and instinctual. For some people, though, the very notion of will is confusing. Whether it's because of an overdose of advertising, peer pressure, or just plain fear, many of us have simply lost touch with what we desire.

True, the more we learn and experience, the more our dreams and expectations evolve. But no matter what stage we're at, each of us has some sense of what our next move in life should be. My contention is this: Everyone (including the Blocked-Heads and the Idea Bunnies) knows instinctively what they'd love to do at any given moment. The problem isn't identifying what their desires are; it's identifying the roots of the fear that prevents them from being wholly present and taking action. Do you remember those blank spaces on the black wall from the beginning of this book? Here's your chance to fill them in.

Brain Bottle Opener 8: The Two-Minute Drill

I want you to take exactly **two minutes** and make a list of things you'd like to do with your life *right now*. Why only two minutes? Because if you give yourself an hour, an afternoon, a day, or a week to create the list, you'll never do it. It won't be happening in the present. Even five minutes can be too long in some cases.

There's a big difference between doing something now and doing something a little later. The present is easy. The present is painless. The immediate present won't let your mind wander off to the refrigerator or the television.

The appearance of your dreams written in actual ink and on actual paper is the first small step toward making them real. One other great thing is that the list of dreams—the list that gets written down somewhere and hangs on the wall behind your computer or on your bathroom mirror—is tantalizing to you and your creative spirit. We're all hungry for our Milky Way Moments, hungry just to know exactly what they are and where we can find them. Here are some of the results of my own Two-Minute Drill:

Scuba diving in Bali
Playing at Carnegie Hall
Watching my daughter get married
Performing in China
Going on a book tour

Lining up dates in Europe for my Big Muse seminar
Learning to fly a plane
Traveling to Eastern Europe with my wife
Learning Spanish
Recording a jazz album
Playing music at a children's hospital
Doing an interview for *The New Yorker*
Buying some land and raising goats and tortoises

It's funny how many surprising things can come out in two minutes. Seeing my daughter's wedding, for example. She doesn't even have a boyfriend that I'm aware of. And this is weird: buying some land and raising goats and tortoises. Now, if I'd had more than two minutes to do this list I'd have probably come up with a host of reasons why that tortoise/goat farm is a stupid, childish, impossible idea. And those are the very reasons that would have prevented most of these ideas from ever coming into the world.

It's not a lack of ideas or the inability to select one perfect idea from among a hundred that holds us back; it's fear of failure and shame and their frightening shadow, fear of abandonment. Whether or not I choose to implement this particular dream of a goat and tortoise farm isn't the point. The point is that by working in the immediacy of the present, I am able to employ some Kid-Thinking to free up my mind to imagine things I might never have considered before. Using the two-minute time limit forces us into the power of the present.

Now it's time for you to write your list. Just write. Don't over-think. Don't even think at all. I want you to list things you've always dreamed of doing but never had the time or the energy or the resources or the courage to actually do. They can be ridiculous things, far-fetched things, ideas that make no sense at all. After you've finished, print out your Two-Minute Drill list, hang it up, and look at it periodically to determine which, if any, of those ideas rings true for you. Again, there's no need to consider how practical the idea is; just see which one, if any, looks most appealing. If you prefer, fold the list and stick it in the back of the book for later.

REAL-WORLD APPLICATIONS

The Two-Minute Drill is the gold mine of the BBO universe. It's the place where you break ground and dredge up new ideas. Some of them (perhaps even most of them) are going to emerge as dirt that needs to be cleaned away, but more often than not, you're going to find something, or learn something of great value. Let's say, for example, that your company has given you a three-month sabbatical to study or write or learn something you've always wanted to try. But instead of being inspired and hopeful, you find that you can't make up your mind about where to apply your focus. Now would be a perfect time to use this BBO.

CHAPTER 9

FUTUREVISION

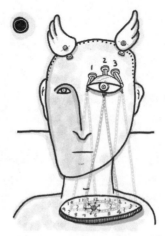

HOW IMAGINING THE SPECIFICS OF A PERFECT FUTURE ENSURES PROPER ACTION IN THE PRESENT

There's an expression I used to hear a lot as a kid: "Think good and it'll be good." I always thought of it as a platitude, some saying meant to give a little hope to a depressed person. Now I see how true it really is. Envisioning something in its complete form even before you begin working on it is how every piece of music, every ballet, every relationship, and every business begins. This ability to see the as-yet-created is what I call FutureVision.

Another powerful way to help quiet negative influences is to use your imagination to create a clear vision of the future you'd like to see for yourself. That vision should include the smallest physical and emotional details: the sounds, the sights, the feelings engendered by the imagined experience. In this chapter we'll read a couple of stories that show how seeing yourself accomplishing your desired goal can play a significant role in producing positive outcomes. We'll also learn some ways to improve and accelerate our own FutureVision.

ONE SUMMER, WHEN I was seventeen, my ability to see was so powerful, it propelled me to a new level of musical and personal engagement.

It was 1977, and I was living in Minneapolis. The air outside was thick as pond water, with an eerie green-sky stillness that signaled an imminent tornado. The calypso band Shangoya was playing, and somewhere between the bone-crushing bass notes and the rhythmic clang of time being beaten out on a rusty brake shoe, I was having an epiphany.

I pictured myself floating outside my body, hovering over the enormous band shell. And as the sun began to set, it was as if I was watching myself on the stage with the band, winding out on my Les Paul. After the show, I gave my phone number to the bass player.

"Your band is good," I said, "but you'd be a whole lot better with me."

Six months later, I got a call. "Shangoya is lookin' for a new guitarist."

The following evening I stood alongside at least a dozen other players waiting to audition, older guys with years of experience and the best equipment. And there I was with this dinky amplifier I'd bought with my bar mitzvah money. Suddenly it was my turn.

"Can you play reggae, mon?" they asked.

I thought back to that image of myself on that stage the night of the tornado watch. I felt like a damn tornado myself. "Hell yeah," I said.

The band started a slow minor-key groove. It was the perfect couch to lay down my raw, bluesy riffs. When the music finally stopped, the band's leader, Aldric Peter Nelson, a lanky Trinidadian with a shaved head and skin the color of molasses, turned to me and said, "What ya tink you can bring to de band if we hire you all jus' now?"

"You see that little amplifier?" I said. "When I'm onstage with you guys—and I will be onstage with you guys—it's gonna shoot flames."

The whole band started laughing at me. I don't blame them. They couldn't help themselves. But in the end, I was the one who got the gig.

SPEECH AND VISION

In rare cases certain individuals pursue and realize their goals as though wearing blinders to all forms of distraction. Their highly detailed FutureVision is so strong that there is almost no interference at all. Sure, they fear criticism, sweat over the outcomes, and harbor some doubts, just like the rest of us. But since they can see themselves succeeding so vividly in their mind's eye, they're seldom susceptible to Marv and his Deflators. They also know that immediately getting engaged in the small, specific steps of what they see in their FutureVision is a most powerful tool in achieving dreams.

My oldest son, Isaac, is that kind of person—at least, he acted like one in his pursuit to become commencement speaker of his graduating class at the University of Massachusetts, Amherst. His speech was chosen from out of a hundred submissions—a huge deal for anyone, but what I recall and why I mention it here is that, at least from a distance, he'd seemed so unafraid and casual about the whole process. When I asked him to think back on what had driven him to write the speech, he told me that it had happened almost at the last minute. He'd received an e-mail announcement reminding students of the due date, and he'd remembered a senior friend of his from sophomore year submitting a speech; Isaac had thought how cool it was that just anyone could try. He'd always considered that delivering the commencement address was something he might like to do, and somehow the e-mail and the due date just made the idea tangible. But the key was what he told me he did next:

"I remember it was a Friday and it was raining, and I went to this coffee shop and I brought some books with me. Anytime I write I always bring books with me, just random books. I like to have words around, especially when I'm writing. It's almost as though the book is a marker saying, 'This is what I'm doing; this is my vision. I'm going to go write and here are some books to prove it.' I watched a handful of speeches online to see what people do. I saw a really good one and it made me think, 'Okay, I'm just gonna start writing it and I'll write it like one of these good ones.' The good ones start off informally. I liked this one where the speaker was sort of self-conscious about giving a commencement speech. I thought it'd be cool to start talking about how I'm about to give a commencement speech, so could we, you know, just get that out of the way. And then I started writing. It was as simple as that. Once I put one word down, it all sort of came out."

Of course, I'm aware that most people don't have that ability to sit down and write without stalling or getting stuck, and I wondered how it just "came out." "Well," Isaac continued, "it's the way I always write any essay. I just write. I think a lot of people approach writing like it's some scary thing. They make the mistake of thinking that you need to slowly construct every sentence individually. At the start, you're just doing stream-of-consciousness writing, like the way you talk. I always write and read out loud to myself as I'm writing, quietly. It just kind of comes out. I know I can always edit and redact later, and that kind of frees me up, I guess. When I finished, I took it and I read it to people. I always do that too."

I wondered whether he had told anyone what he was going to do (as he'd mentioned it to me in passing, over the phone one day). And if so, who else had he told and why? Isaac explained it like this: "I told a lot of people. If you don't tell anyone, the stakes are too low. Low stakes means low pressure. Low pressure often means something won't ever get done."

What Isaac did was something we've touched on already. You might think putting extra pressure on yourself by telling people your intention is counterproductive, but as we've seen, it has the effect of making a goal more real. As Isaac put it: "If you never say what you're about to do—literally say it out loud—it doesn't really exist." Just as we saw with the Smartphone Letter BBO, what you think or feel is an act of creation but it doesn't become manifest until you literally or metaphorically *hit Send*!

It's not that Isaac didn't doubt himself or have second thoughts throughout the process; he confided that he did. It's what he did that kept the doubts at bay—what he did without even thinking about it at the time—that is so relevant to us all. He practiced giving the speech to his roommate over and over, an act that was more than mere preparation. By delivering the speech in practice, he was ingraining the feeling of giving the speech at the commencement; he was creating a sensory reality of the event before that reality even existed. And the result? He saw all the specifics. He saw himself up there. He saw the effect his speech would have on people. And he began to truly believe that he and nobody else should give this speech. As he put it: "Once you set out to do something, fear is turned into something else. When you've taken action you've already conquered the fear. In my case, I told people that I was going to write the speech. I had a friend, a girl who told me after the fact that she'd wanted to write the speech. But she hadn't said anything until after the due date—when it was too late. It was self-sabotage. She didn't want to get rejected, so she didn't mention it. Instead of saying, 'I submitted it but I didn't get chosen,' now she can always use the excuse of, 'Oh yeah, I just missed the due date. I never got around to doing it.' I always had the feeling that she felt pacified somehow by simply believing she might have been chosen had she only tried."

How often do we allow ourselves to be pacified by a lack of FutureVision? The word *pacified*, as it happens, perfectly describes the way we are sometimes left momentarily infantilized by fear, content to toddle about with a baby's paci in our mouths. It's cute when we're small and helpless—when it's appropriate. Not so cute when we're adults. If our FutureVision is lacking, it's almost certain that we'll miss out on our Milky Way Moments and wind up pacified but disappointed. But when we picture ourselves achieving a

Isaac Himmelman delivering the commencement speech at the University of Massachusetts, Amherst

goal, articulate the desire of that goal, and take action through simple and practical steps that are immediate and true, more often than not we move closer to creating our envisioned reality.

Brain Bottle Opener 9: FutureVision

Imagine it's precisely three years from this very moment. Where are you? Who are you with? What are you doing? How is your health? What are you working on? What is your mood? Exactly what do you see outside your window?

Take **five minutes** to write this all down. It's important to include as much detail as possible. Consider no detail too small.

Be free to see yourself happy and successful in this exercise. I've done this BBO over the years with friends and I've seen how the people who paint their futures in muted tones of browns and grays all seem to wind up living in a world of brown and gray. Go ahead and paint a vibrant, color-filled future for yourself.

Remember, this is a place where you're not going to be judged on your accuracy. In other words, this is not the time to try and be overly realistic. I did this BBO on the advice of my mother when I was twenty-two, and I'm amazed at how much of what I wrote, though far-fetched at the time, has come true today.

REAL-WORLD APPLICATIONS

This BBO is perfect to try when you find yourself in transition. Perhaps you've just graduated from college and are looking to start your career. Perhaps you're in between jobs or just looking for a change of direction. Creating a FutureVision statement will help you home in on a time far ahead of you. And most important, the knowledge that you gain will help you discover the best first steps to take on that journey toward new possibilities.

CHAPTER 10

STAYING TRUE

FINDING AND LISTENING TO YOUR OWN CREATIVE VOICE

The reason I chose the Why You statement as the first BBO of this book is because a major test for anyone truly pursuing a dream is to determine what he or she stands for. If you're doing something connected with your deepest values, the odds are you'll be able to see it through to the finish. That question of what we stand for should be simple but it's not. Our beliefs are constantly challenged by multibillion-dollar industries devoted to telling us what we should wear, who we should pay attention to, and what we should strive to become (usually a more active consumer). The accumulated result of this values-poison is that it's easy to lose sight of who we are and what we're striving for.

Consider how many slogans and ad taglines over the years have incorporated quasi-spiritual words into their messaging: Dream, Soar, Imagine, "There is no substitute," "It's the real thing." Advertising is designed to inspire, but too often in the process of speaking to our aspirations, it reminds us of what we're lacking—that we're overweight, in pain, aging, and out of style. If we were more attuned to our Big Muse, we might not hear the negative messaging in a way that reinforces our worst images of ourselves. How would speaking to our desires as opposed to our fears change the face of advertising? The reason certain advertisers address our fears so often is because most of us are far more familiar with them than we are with our truest objectives. Fear is popular and predictable when it comes to sales. The longer we can stay inauthentic, the better for them.

But while you can always fake something, the question is, for how long? You can marry a woman you don't truly love; you can take a job for the money; you can write a song you don't like just because you think it'll be popular. But sooner or later, you'll wish you had done something that you really felt like doing, something that expressed your desire and not just your fear of doing something that people might deem childish or unreasonable. How many times have you been afraid to speak your mind or follow your Big Muse because you were afraid of the reactions of others? Bill Watterson, the creator of the popular comic strip *Calvin and Hobbes*, captures this idea beautifully:

> Creating a life that reflects your values and satisfies your soul is a rare achievement. In a culture that relentlessly promotes avarice and excess as the good life, a person happy doing his own work is usually considered an eccentric, if not a subversive. Ambition is only understood if it's to rise to the top of some imaginary ladder of success.

Oftentimes being true to our FutureVision means finding that our outlook on life is completely at odds with that of the people around us. Breaking free of their expectations for how we should live often takes a great deal of courage. It also demands that we take action on something that we believe in, something that reflects and manifests our truest values. Holding dissenting opinions is difficult and most of us will simply choose to avoid upsetting the status quo. The choice is always ours. We can stay with the dried-grass eaters or we can take steps to get to our personal Milky Way Moment. In this chapter we will meet someone who clearly did the latter.

THE PERSPECTIVE OF BIRDS

One Sunday morning a family friend invited Josh Rabinowitz to take a short flight from the Santa Monica airport. He was nine years old. They took to the skies in a single-engine Cessna and flew out over the flat blue expanse of the Pacific, and he was hooked. After that day Josh dreamed of becoming a commercial pilot. But despite knowing exactly what he wanted for his future, he grew up believing that his dreams were hopeless. First, there was the huge technical challenge of learning to fly, but beyond that, Josh had to defy the wishes of his parents, who had an entirely different set of plans for him. Here's the story of a young man who found that the keys that unlocked his dream went beyond a particular skill set, self-discipline, or abundant resources; in the end it had only to do with the truth of his desire.

Josh's father is an Orthodox rabbi and both he and Josh's mother had strict views about Josh's future. They involved Josh going to Jewish day school, and then after eighth grade, going to yeshiva (religious school), and then becoming a rabbi himself, getting married, and having a big family. In no uncertain terms, his parents told him, "This is what you're going to do." Becoming a commercial pilot most definitely didn't fit into that plan. So I asked him, "What was the step you took that made you realize becoming a pilot was a possibility?" And as it turned out, it boiled down to a conversation he'd had with his sister.

"At the time I was in yeshiva in Israel," he said. "I think I was eighteen at this point, and the program I was in wasn't working out for me. I had little to no interest in leading that kind of life and the only reason I went was because I was basically forced to. During a phone call with my sister she asked me what I was going to do with my life when school was over. It was then that I realized the one thing I wanted to do, the only thing I wanted to do, was to become a pilot and I told her so. She told me, 'You have a passion; you need to go for it.'"

It's funny how simple many of our needs really are. All Josh had ever really needed was to have just one family member say that his dream was permissible. Those few but important words gave him the courage to look into flight schools and ultimately to confront his father. And as is often the case in such situations in which Marv has devoted years to building up our fears, working the Deflators around the clock to dramatize our expectation of how such a conversation might play out (like a Greek tragedy, of course), the reality can seem anticlimactic. Sure, mustering the courage to slay a dragon and then discovering that the dragon is actually a grasshopper lacks the dramatic payoff of a final showdown. It's not the explosive ending the Deflators would have written. But make no mistake—it is the best possible ending you could hope for. Realizing that you're free to pursue your dream, however big or small, is a revelation. As it happened, Josh approached his father, told him his dream, and asked for his help in getting a student loan. After a few days of conversation, his father not only acquiesced, but he became a vigorous supporter.

I asked Josh, "Now that you had your family's backing, did you ever doubt your ability—did you think that you could somehow fail at achieving your dream?"

"Absolutely," he said. "I didn't have a normal high school education. I had to pass my GED and I knew that was going to be hard because my math skills were pretty weak. I also didn't feel confident when I signed up for the flight training. But once I committed, dropping out wasn't an option for me. I kept saying to myself, 'If you screw this up, you're not going to become a pilot, which is what you want for your life.' That's why giving up wasn't an option. I just felt like: 'I will rise to this opportunity.'"

At the time of this writing Josh is living in San Juan, Puerto Rico, flying for a small aviation company. He is logging hours with them until he's got enough to get a job with a major carrier. In his words, "The job is a stepping-stone." But he also said, "There are moments just around sunset, when I'm flying over the Caribbean and I can clearly feel that all the struggles I've had were worth the effort."

Brain Bottle Opener 10: Rewrite

Think back to one occasion when you completely caved in to someone else's expectations for how you should have acted or felt in a given situation.

Perhaps you went along with a group who was bad-mouthing someone who didn't deserve it. Maybe you were asked to do something you felt was beneath your dignity or even immoral. Perhaps you did something beneath your standards just for the money.

Now, take **five minutes** and using that same scenario, write another outcome for yourself. Rewrite that episode as if you'd acted exactly as you'd wished.

REAL-WORLD APPLICATIONS

This BBO is great for those times when you feel that regret is holding you back from succeeding in a new leadership role. Let's say you've been given the opportunity to manage a team of fifty people. You're excited about the possibilities, but you find yourself ruminating on a time in your life when you buckled under pressure. Maybe you even did something dishonest or otherwise lacking in integrity. The Rewrite will help you see that while you may have acted poorly, the negative action you took is not the essence of who you are. It will show you that your capacity for growth is still very much alive.

Knowing that you can change, and in fact have just changed by rewriting your past, will give you renewed strength to proceed as a leader.

PART THREE REVIEW

LET'S PAUSE A moment and look back on what you've learned in this section.

- You completed the Two-Minute Drill and made a list of things you'd love to do. In the process, you suspended common sense (not always a good idea, but certainly important on occasion) to better understand the kinds of things that make you happy. Having a clear idea of what you desire, whether it's obtainable or not, is reassuring to Marv. We know that when he's happy, we're happy.
- Using your FutureVision, you created a detailed picture of yourself engaged in the joyous pursuit of your dream. Now, after doing this, you can actually see yourself there. Reinforcing this vision of *you* in the midst of your dream is one of your most important tools. The order to dream-making is this: First you form a vision of the ephemeral idea, and afterward you have the actual experience of it becoming manifest.

- And finally you've done the Rewrite, in which you revised those times in your past when you compromised on your values. Rewriting an old scenario like this is a form of forgiveness. Just as when you forgive others, forgiving yourself releases you from Marv's main source of energy: negativity. With little energy, he'll naturally take a long nap and leave you alone to create.

These initial actions of establishing a dream and envisioning it realized (as a form of gauging its true meaning) are the closely connected keys to achieving any creative goal you set for yourself. Whether it's taking on a new project at work, launching a company, or looking to deepen a relationship with someone you love, if you implement the three BBOs in Part Three, you will start down a path toward manifesting your dream. And best of all, it only takes a few minutes to do them.

In this next part, let's look at some of the potential challenges you're going to face in maintaining your enthusiasm along this path.

PART FOUR

THE PATH

We don't receive wisdom; we must discover it for ourselves after a journey that no one can take for us or spare us.

-Marcel Proust

CHAPTER 11

THE BACKACHE OF CHANGE

COPING WITH TRANSITION AND EMBRACING THE NEW

In his 1970 opus on the dangers of rapid change, *Future Shock* author Alvin Toffler wrote: "Change is avalanching upon our heads and most people are grotesquely unprepared to cope with it." "Unprepared" is an understatement when unwelcome changes happen to us on a personal level. When they do it's not academic, not just something we've read about or heard about; it truly feels like an avalanche. The following is an account of my own mini-avalanche.

GREEN LUMBAR CHAIRS AND THE BACKACHE OF FORCED CHANGE

My wife and I had recently finished remodeling our home, incurring all sorts of bills as the costs went careering past the contractor's original estimate. At around the same time, I got a phone call to come down to Fox Studios in West Los Angeles the following day to interview for a job as composer for a new television show, which included writing the theme song and all the musical underscore. The call came just as I'd written a studio design firm an ungodly large check for doing the last of the wiring in my recording studio, and my thinking at the time was that the meeting couldn't have come at a more auspicious moment. As it turned out, the meeting went well and I was awarded the position the day of the interview. And so, in late August of 1999 I started working on a new TV series called *Judging Amy*, which eventually ran on CBS for six seasons.

I'd done some television work in the past but this was the first big network show I'd worked on. Even though becoming a television composer had never been my goal, the job was something I believed I really wanted. I had four young kids, and traveling as a working rock musician kept me away from them and my wife. And besides, the money the show was offering was far better than what I'd been taking home from my work on the road.

There was one more thing that, ironically, made it attractive: I had a certain degree of doubt and fear about whether or not I could do this kind of work, and that challenge alone got me excited. Meeting the writers, actors, and producers and seeing them so enthusiastic to have a real rock musician scoring their show made me feel important and valued.

I was anxious, of course, but since I had to dive immediately into the work of learning the highly technical process of scoring a network television show, I was more engaged in the work than in the worry. But I found that as I became more and more comfortable with the process of making music for the show, I was less challenged creatively. As the show progressed into the second and third seasons, I no longer had to dig as deep to find new ideas. It seemed I had my TV composer's road map laid out in front of me and there was very little call from any of the show's producers for me to venture off it. But instead of enjoying the easier ride, I was finding myself feeling less and less engaged in the work itself, and given the human need to feel like something more than an automaton, that easier ride just invited more self-doubt. I always tried to be professional about creating the best music I possibly could, but somewhere around the end of the show's fourth season I got to a point where I felt like I was turning out what amounted to musical widgets and collecting a paycheck. Now, I understand how some people might think that would be a good thing, some way to make some easy money. But the fact is, true creativity and, most important, creativity's consequent joys, don't exist in habit; they exist in change and in challenge.

Devising a process that's effortless and cost-effective might seem like a worthy goal, but for creative work, the reality is that the innovative spirit shuts down when our jobs become mechanized. Lacking new avenues for inspired expression causes us to become bored, and it wasn't long before that boredom I was experiencing caused a mild depression.

FROM THAT POINT it was just Marv and me wrestling together on a daily basis for almost a decade, through my work on shows like

Judging Amy, Making the Band, Bug Juice, Men in Trees, and several others. Here's what happened the day everything changed.

I was sitting in my green lumbar support chair watching a scene from *Bones*. The chair has collapsible arms that allow me to play my guitar without banging into them (I've spent hundreds, maybe thousands of hours in this chair). I was staring at my computer monitor. The scene I was working on was supposed to seem scary but it wasn't. It just felt empty. My job was to add the emotion. For this music cue I wanted a huge drum sound that throbbed along the bottom of the track, something deep; an Indian dhol, perhaps. I wanted it to sound impossibly big, so I dialed in some digital reverb that rang out for six full seconds. Now the drum sounded as if it was being played in a massive cave. Next, I played some discordant piano notes, after that some dark cello lines, and then a high-pitched tremolo violin that sounded like a human scream. I turned up the volume, pushed back my chair, and listened as the music played against the picture. The scene was actually scary now and everything seemed alive.

I had been doing this kind of work without a break for more than ten years. I was grateful for the job, but somehow I'd always imagined that I'd be playing my own songs onstage and getting paid for them. I fantasized about quitting, taking a stab at resurrecting my performance career, but the money was too good, and besides, I just didn't have the brass down inside my pouch that I used to.

That afternoon I got a call from Donald, the postproduction supervisor of the show. Since the writers and producers who had originally hired me had begun work on other projects, Donald was the guy assigned to give me notes on the music I composed. Lately, the sound of his voice had become so irritating that I'd asked him to leave his comments on my answering machine rather than speaking with me directly (never a good sign).

In that evening's message, Donald requested that I come into the studio for a scheduling meeting the next morning. "What the hell is a scheduling meeting?" I asked myself. "And why can't it be done over the phone?" I got to the studio around noon and waited for Donald in his office. When he arrived he was as lighthearted as I'd ever seen him. "Let's go upstairs to Jim's office," he said.

At that moment, I thought I knew what lambs must feel like when they're about to be slaughtered. It wasn't as tense as you might think. Mostly, it was a sense of resignation, of bowing to the inevitable as the blade comes down.

"Peter, you've been doing a great job; we're just . . . looking for a change."

Minutes later I walked out into the parking lot, my eyes adjusting to the harsh light of a Southern California afternoon, feeling the dread of finally getting what I thought I wanted. Half of me was saying, "You're free!" The other was saying, "You're screwed!"

WHY IS IT that we so often see challenge and confusion as obstacles to overcome? We strive to figure things out in an effort to make our lives simpler, as though "easy" is the reward, when in fact the absence of challenge and confusion more times than not reflects an absence of creativity. Learning curves can be hard and at times overwhelming, but the opposite—and routines are just that—is boring!

Reinventing yourself is scary stuff, but change has a way of fueling our creativity. True, we avoid it because we're pained by it so often, but we must strive to absorb this axiom: *Change is not only inevitable; it's fundamental to living creatively.* The troubling part is that oftentimes, we're not even aware that change is taking place. While I was sitting in that green lumbar chair scoring those TV shows, I had no idea how many upheavals were about to commence. How could I? I was too busy going through the motions, doing the day-to-day work. Certainly, when catastrophic accidents and illnesses occur we can't help being shocked awake. But what I'm referring to are those times when we're on autopilot without once realizing that we have the power not only to take notice of change, but to use it to improve the way we're currently living. Becoming aware of the currents of change means getting out of our own heads and taking a break from our own biases and habitual behaviors. Sharing time with friends, experiencing nature, and being significantly helpful to others in need can help wake us up to the silent fluctuations going on around us. Experiencing something radically new is perhaps the best way to become reinvigorated.

While it's true that change often comes as a result of things we couldn't possibly have imagined, just as frequently, it arrives as a result of things we've done to bring it about. If you're like me, you regularly look back on changes such as losing a job, divorce, or even the angry dissolution of a rock band with an I'm-not-at-fault view. Circumstances or someone else's actions are always to blame. "Not me!" we say, and always with great certainty.

In the past, when I thought back on some of the backaching transitions I've had to endure, I made those same excuses. I now see that there was very little serious thought given to how I was personally responsible for the way things turned out. Many of my most difficult periods of change had to do with mistakes I'd made that I was either not brave enough to admit to or too blind to see. Several years ago I went on a journey of sorts into my own mind to discover some things about the way I deal with change. Among other things, I noticed I have a very difficult time with it.

We have a way of blinding ourselves to the actions we've taken that have led to our contractions, or failures, if you prefer the term. But by uncovering the profound yet subtle thought patterns that prevent us from seeing the ways we've been at fault in many situations both personally and professionally, we will be able to better understand the way our minds work and our own tendency toward self-sabotage. And though it's not a panacea, armed with this new knowledge about ourselves, we will be equipped to work with and relate to people in a way that's more relaxed, more joyous, and more productive.

Brain Bottle Opener II: Acknowledgment Is Knowledge

In this BBO I want you to take **six minutes** to write about an episode in which you were wholly or partly responsible for creating painful change in your life.

Think about a time you had (up until this moment) blamed something or someone other than yourself for a problem you were experiencing. You could be thinking back to a divorce, a business venture that went bad, or a break with a friend or family member.

Just as an example, let's take one more look at the time I got fired. Here's what I wrote about my part in causing the event. It illustrates exactly what I'm talking about:

I can talk all I want about Donald and his annoying personality. The truth is, he had a difficult job and all the direction he was giving me about my music was simply something he thought he needed to do. Rather than perceive it all as an affront to my ego—which I basically did—I should have been much more mindful about his challenging role. He was given so much responsibility by the producers and so little decision-making power. That would drive anyone mad. Knowing that and being empathetic to Donald's situation should have made me more attuned to the need to foster better communication with him. Instead, I wound up humiliating him by making him leave his notes on my answering machine.

Had I taken him out to lunch even once in three years? No. Did I have even one personal conversation with him? No. Had I ever acknowledged the herculean effort he was putting forth for the show? Nope. No wonder that when I needed an ally, someone on the inside to speak up for me, Donald was probably the first to say, "Give him the boot."

In hindsight I see how easily I could have remedied the situation, yet because of my arrogance, I did nothing but retreat.

REAL-WORLD APPLICATIONS

This BBO is helpful when you find yourself coming around to a similar challenging circumstance for a second or third time. For example, let's say you've vowed that when your wife criticizes you, you'll refrain from snapping back at her and exacerbating the situation. Now it's happening again. But by doing the Acknowledgment Is Knowledge BBO, you've given yourself an opportunity to exercise one of the most important mental muscles we humans have: our capacity for empathy. When those muscles are strengthened, we will have a much easier time being empathetic to the needs of others, and as a result we'll be much better at controlling our tempers and our egos. From a practical standpoint, this will allow us to make more reasoned decisions in the future.

CHAPTER 12

EXPLODING THE LOGJAMS

BREAKING WITH THE PAST
TO UNLOCK THE FUTURE

One of the central prayers in Judaism comes at the start of the Yom Kippur holiday; it's called the Kol Nidre. Its melody is both mournful and stately. On its face, the prayer is a no-nonsense declaration:

> We hereby consider any vows and oaths we have taken this past year to be null and void.

Such terse legal language would seem like a very unpoetic way of ushering in the holiness of that sacred day. But in essence, it's a stunning metaphor that says: To look at ourselves as new and pure spirits, we must begin by cutting our connection (our vows) to the demoralizing, dehumanizing experiences of our past.

We all have a tendency to hold on to our memories, the good ones and the challenging ones. It's possible, though, that we fear that by letting go of them—even the memories that do need letting go of—we will somehow lose something of ourselves, something of our pasts, and be diminished by the loss. The truth is closer to this: We become more ourselves when we relieve ourselves of painful memories. Letting go of pain and anger is like cleaning the lens of a camera. When we relax our grasp on our challenging past experiences, our FutureVision improves. We don't let go entirely—that's not possible—but we can learn to set down the pain and the anger. By releasing our grip, we don't let go of the memory; we let go of the lack of clarity that memory can inflict.

IMAGINE A RIVER that usually runs fast and deep. It's an artery through which flows all sorts of things: fish, boats, endless amounts of water, and logs from the mill thirty miles upstream. It sometimes happens that there are so many logs in the river at one time that they form an inadvertent dam. Some of the logs turn sideways, others catch on rocks and debris in the water, and before you know it, there's a massive pileup in the middle of the river and nothing can get through. Sometimes the logjam gets so bad that the only solution is to use dynamite to blow the whole thing apart and allow the water to flow again.

Those months after losing my job on *Bones* were some of the most depressing I'd had in years. I was stuck in a rut with no clue how to free myself, or what I'd go on to do if I could. There were so many things I could have been accomplishing. Writing a song, learning how to fly a plane, working on this book . . . The trouble was that there was an anchor weighing me down, dragging me farther and farther away from my aspirations. My mind was jammed full, not of ideas but of reasons—good ones too—about why everything I wanted to do wasn't worth doing.

Bob Nordeman, a good friend and mentor of mine, once said, "A rut is a grave with both ends kicked out."

A "grave" is a dramatic way of describing it, but the metaphor is apt. Being stuck in a rut, I felt dead inside, unable to make decisions, unable to move forward or back. The rock star business I had long dreamed of being a part of had atrophied. I had to start letting go of my old dreams and search for new ones. It wasn't easy.

I mention this to you to point out that just because a life choice no longer works for us, it doesn't mean we haven't formed incredibly strong attachments to it. In my case, it seemed impossible to give up what I'd worked so long to create (my recording career and even my career as a television composer). Even though I no longer saw those things as totally feasible, I still had strong attachments to them.

I was stuck in a no-man's land, not knowing exactly who I had become or where I was going. I was experiencing the Logjam. Any forward progress would necessitate a ton of TNT.

But how do you blow up your own Logjam without burning down the forest around it? How do you explode the grief, the dissatisfaction, and the sheer exhaustion that prevents you from even imagining a better future without hurting those around you? That was a question I should have been asking myself a long time ago, had I been self-aware enough to even notice the changes going on around me and inside.

CLEARING THE LOGJAM

Clearing a Logjam requires that you understand, as transparently as possible, the underlying causes of your negative states of mind. That's why it's so critical that you learn to recognize the way your mind works.

The degree to which you can understand, acknowledge, and observe your own motivations is the degree to which you will succeed in clearing your Logjam. One of the things I eventually did to clear mine was to write myself a detailed document called a Letting Go Letter. In it, I described everything I could remember about what had led me to my contracted mental state in the first place.

I've included a section of the actual Letting Go Letter I wrote to myself that difficult summer of 2011.

> I need to let go of a sense that I will be in danger if I am truly myself. My biggest fear is that I will be unloved if I reveal my true self. In fact, I may well lose certain people, but that's far different from being in real danger, and if I lose them because I've acted honestly, of what value are they to me anyway? But what does being myself even entail? The first thing that comes to mind is to be brave enough to state the truth as I see it. Perhaps I'm too sensitive to the feelings of others and so, in trying to protect them, I hesitate to speak my mind. But even as I write this, I know it's crap. I know it's only me I'm trying to protect, no one else. I often believe that speaking my mind, asking for

what I need, will lead to that need going unanswered. The threat of not being answered, of not being responded to, signals a kind of grave threat.

At some point when I was very small I somehow took on the idea that a mind-set of self-denial was the pathway to my survival. Now that thought and mode of behavior has become so ingrained it's nearly impossible to change. Losing this fear would be a significant help in finding out where I stand and where I need to go next. Right now, as I have for several years, I feel as though I'm in the middle of a search: unsettled, undetermined, without having any hope of an arrival.

THE "I" INSIDE us always perceives itself as being apart from the rest of the world, something separate with an unfailing sense of its own uniqueness. Our five senses are the best ways (currently the only ways—though that may well change) we have of interfacing with the world beyond ourselves. It is that engagement with the outside that stimulates and allows for what we typically call inspiration. And inspiration is the TNT that invariably blows apart the Logjams. When we're "stuck" it's often because we've become too separated from the world around us. It's because we've found ourselves living too much inside our own heads, half-drunk with the sound of our own habits, biases, and fears. Here are some simple ideas that have helped me break out of mine:

- **Visit a children's hospital.** You can volunteer to read stories or play music or do a puppet show. Being in this highly charged environment is profound and it will shake you out of your own head. Have a look around at the faces of the children, but more important, take a look at the parents. They're confused, stricken, and full of fear. This is where you'll restore your empathy, your hope, and even your imagination. We all tend to think of ourselves as sympathetic, sensitive folks, though the truth is, very often we find ourselves rather selfishly locked away in our private, overly intellectualized vacuums. A visit of this nature is guaranteed to pull you out.

- **Listen to music.** Shut off the lights, shut off the phone, shut your eyes, and listen to music for twenty minutes. Curtis Mayfield, Howlin' Wolf, Paul Hindemith, Claude Debussy, the Replacements—all work wonders for releasing the Big Muse. It doesn't matter what you listen to, but it is important to close your eyes and, if you're able, let the music form visual patterns behind your eyelids. Setting aside time and devoting it exclusively to listening is key, with the sound waves from the outside entering your mind on the inside.

- **Exercise.** Moving in any way you prefer is perfect. Personally, I like to box. The adrenaline of someone dancing around in front of me and trying to punch me in the head or the stomach immediately takes me out of myself. Running, swimming, walking, and dancing are great too; it matters only that you do something every day that makes you sweat.

- **Pray.** I can't stress this enough. Being constantly in touch with whatever your conception is of a force bigger than yourself is vital to maintaining a sense of humility, a sense of proportion, and a sense that you are not alone in your challenges. I'm not talking about organized religion, necessarily. I'm talking about deep, meaningful, and personal prayer. That is, asking for help in your own words, as a child beseeches a parent. Speaking of asking for help:

- **Ask for help.** This is so obvious, we're inclined to miss it altogether. Call a friend, a relative, or a therapist to help you see your problem in a new light. I know so many people who, in the interest of projecting an image of self-sufficiency, go for months or even years without allowing someone to shed some objectivity on their issues. Don't be one of these people. Pick up the phone and schedule a walk or a lunch where you can talk and a friend can listen. Don't be worried about being a burden. No one's going to see you as that, especially if you're already reluctant to do this.

Finally, when you've built enough bridges between yourself and the world outside you'll find yourself more inspired, energized, and ready to get back to living. The great irony is that with the new inspiration, what we naturally do next is go deep inside ourselves again, dig around to discover new ideas, and then start the cycle all over. Expect this as a natural pattern. You may feel inspired for a while, working with abandon, and then slightly depressed afterward—although the more you're aware of this progression, the less severe the swings are likely to be.

Anyone who tells you he or she can free you from this cycle needs to be cautiously attended to. Creativity demands our doubts and our frustrations. It insists that we run up against a wall that appears impossible to climb, that we experience the occasional

Logjam. Our resources are marshaled when we are challenged. There's simply no way around this. One thing that's always helpful is to take notice of the fluctuating mental states you go through. Be the observer. See yourself being pulled into negative emotional states. When you do, you can more easily stop yourself from being pulled any further.

As I've mentioned, there's a beat, a split second, in which you are conscious of the pull. You can arrest the slide in that very moment. If you miss it, it'll be just a bit more difficult to pull yourself out than if you hadn't fallen in at all, but still possible. The longer you are consumed by the negative emotions, the harder it will be to climb out. It's all about that split second when you can still see yourself sliding in. See if you can let the anger pass as effortlessly as you might let the trees on the side of the road pass as you drive by. It takes practice but you'll get better and better at it with time.

Brain Bottle Opener 12: Letting Go Letter

This is a letter that you write to yourself describing all the things in your life you need to let go of, things you are carrying that serve no positive purpose at all.

The Letting Go Letter works best when you list the sounds, the tactile sensations, the smells, the tastes, the sights—all the minutiae of what you feel needs letting go of. Don't forget to include a detailed depiction of your emotional state and the emotional state of the people closest to you.

If you need help, look back at my own example earlier in the chapter. Now give yourself **ten minutes** to write this letter, and place it where you can see it every morning for at least one week.

REAL-WORLD APPLICATIONS

Use the Letting Go Letter whenever you feel you're in a rut. For example, you might be a new mother or father experiencing guilt about your conflicted feelings. On the one hand, you've never loved anything or anyone as much as this new baby of yours. On the other hand (and though you're loath to admit it), there is so much about the constant caregiving that feels overwhelming. Doing this particular BBO right now will give you the perspective that you clearly require. Perhaps you need to let go of your expectations for what the whole parenting experience was going to be like. Perhaps you need to let go of your assumptions about exactly what constitutes being a "good" mother or father. Whatever ideas you come up with, there's no question that releasing them from your subconscious and into your conscious mind is going to give you new insight and therefore some benefit.

CHAPTER 13

FILTERS VS. DOORWAYS

HOW TO MAKE THE MIND A DOORWAY RATHER THAN A FILTER AT THE BEGINNING OF A CREATIVE PROCESS

It's often thought that the brain's main function is to take in information. In fact, a crucial role of our brains is to filter out information so that we're not overwhelmed with input. This is called "selective attention" and it's based on the work of psychologists George Miller and Donald Broadbent in the 1950s. Miller in particular discovered that primary memory (which is the information we are currently aware of or thinking about) could hold "seven plus or minus two" items at the same time. More than that and it gets very difficult. To better illustrate this, look at seven objects around you right now. Then, go into another room and quickly write them all down. Next, take those same seven objects and try to eliminate two of them from your mind. It's like trying to stop thinking of a pink elephant after someone puts the idea into your head.

To interact effectively with the world around us, our brains must process overwhelming amounts of complex information. Since the brain can carry out only a limited number of tasks at a time, it has to select the most relevant information, based on our needs at any given moment. The prefrontal cortex determines what information is to be given priority and which cognitive resources are needed to analyze this information and eliminate distractions. This is how we're able to concentrate on one conversation at a time at a busy diner.

Certain situations require us to quickly analyze the world around us. Various areas of the brain come into play, depending on the type of stimuli: sights, smells, sounds, touch, and tastes. You'd need this sort of selective attention if you had to find a red crayon in a drawer full of random objects, for example. If you were looking for your mother in a crowd, you'd use your selective visuospatial functions, in the upper central part of the brain, to select her face from all others.

In terms of creativity, however, we find that this selective attention often becomes disruptive because it doesn't allow the right brain (thought to be the creative hemisphere) to wander off and make its nonlinear, uncommon connections. The ability to temporarily reduce the effects of selective attention is an important step in increasing our knack for thinking creatively.

Though we can vastly improve our access to creativity, it isn't a skill per se. Let's be sure not to confuse creativity with mastery. They're not the same. One is a normal human condition and the other is something acquired through years of training. Think of creativity as a natural force like gravity or the movement of the planets. Eliminate fear, and creativity begins to appear. It's that simple. Creativity, which is the ability to be fully present and adaptive to challenges and stimuli, exists in all of us; it is a natural part of us. Of course, if it's so native to the human experience, then why is it in evidence in some people much more than others, and why does it often feel so distant? Simply put, it's because certain people have habituated themselves to processes and practices that can unlock their creative minds.

From a neurological point of view, the brain is more a filter, or a sieve, than an open door. Therefore, training the mind to be less limiting in what it allows to enter can help expand our access to creativity. As I've just pointed out, one of the brain's main functions is to be selective about where we focus our attention. Because it blocks out so much input, there is always much more sensory input left behind than absorbed. How else would we function while bombarded with the millions of sensory perceptions we are presented with at any given moment? That said, in order to foster a greater grasp of our own intrinsic creativity, we need a method to decrease the excessive activity of the filtration system that the brain provides us with. We need techniques that allow a greater degree of willingness on the part of the brain to admit stimuli it might normally reject.

For instance, if you're sitting at your computer trying to write a business proposal and you're drawing a blank, it might be helpful to focus momentarily on things that your brain has rejected. *The sound of the rain outside. The smell of the coffee in your cup. A glint of sunlight hitting your desk from a nearby window. A cobweb in the corner of the ceiling.* It's not that there needs to be any direct correlation to what you're working on. That's not the important idea. What is important is that for a fleeting moment, by noticing the things your brain has filtered out, you allow it to relax its propensity to stop the flow of information, diminishing its natural selective tendency. That way it can provide you with a greater willingness to accept ideas you might otherwise reject or neglect. That's why so many of us have our most powerful revelations in the shower. The warm water on our naked skin, the smell of the soap, and the sound of the water cause our analytical minds to take a break and our sensory perceptions to predominate.

In one example of this phenomenon, a study published in the *Journal of Consumer Research* shows that the best work space for creative projects should contain some background noise. Ravi Mehta, a researcher at the University of Illinois at Urbana-Champaign, and his team tested the effects of extraneous noise on participants' creative thinking skills. During the experiment participants were separated into four groups and asked to complete a commonly used measurement of creative thinking called the Remote Associates Test, in which test takers are asked to look for relationships between a series of words that appear unrelated. Each group was given different levels of white and pink background noise at 50 decibels (dB), 70 dB, 85 dB, and total silence while taking the test. To give you a sense of what that sounded like, white noise is artificially generated and sounds like a gentle hissing. Pink noise is synthetic as well, and it sounds something like the static on an untuned television channel.

After scoring the results, the researchers found that those in the 70 dB group (described as a moderate level of ambient noise) significantly outperformed those in the other three groups. The extraneous sensory information (in this case, the background noise) was a boon to their creative thinking. You don't want too much stimulus—that just becomes a distraction—but having none at all inhibits creativity. This is why you find so many people typing away on their laptops in bustling coffee shops. There's even an app called Coffitivity, which simulates the sounds of a coffee shop to help generate creativity.

FIGHT, FLIGHT, AND SHUTTERING THE SHADES TO POSSIBILITIES

The brain has another astounding function. The limbic brain (specifically the amygdala), which has been called the primitive brain and the emotional brain, is constantly on the lookout for life-threatening danger. (Sounds a lot like Marv, doesn't it?) The most primitive part of our brains from an evolutionary perspective is located deep in the temporal lobe; it consists of several subregions having to do with different aspects of perception, information gathering, and regulating emotions such as fear and love. If we were walking down the street and an angry dog suddenly growled at us from behind a fence, the amygdala would cause us to breathe in involuntarily. That inhalation would provide a quick burst of oxygen, allowing us to run or fight. Interestingly, the limbic brain reacts in a similar way to nonphysical threats, such as criticism of our ideas or even the perception of criticism. On some deep emotional level we often perceive censure as a sort of life-threatening danger.

The capacity for absorbing knowledge and information is arguably at its peak in infants and young children. Studies have shown that humans as young as five months are cognizant in some way of their own fragility, of their need to be nurtured and guarded. If there were a suspicion or a sense that our parents might somehow reject us, that suspicion would lead to increased anxiety. The anxiety would arise because, as I've mentioned, we somehow understood that rejection at that early stage in our lives would mean death. To be sure, there's no way we had all this clearly reasoned as infants, but it's likely that the powerful amygdala had (and still has) a way of intuiting this kind of danger. It's no different from the reaction it has at the growling of the angry dog. Fear of rejection and fear of angry dogs are both instinctual reactions to a perceived mortal danger. As a result, that rush of fear often triggers selective attention, which, as we know, is a limiting of input and possibilities. In a time of danger, the amygdala creates those limits because we need our minds to focus on immediate threats, not on poetry or music.

In a similar vein, our innate fear of shame is also strong, and as a result, we tend to limit our creative options when we feel we're being judged. By now we understand that fear of judgment is, at its root, a fear of abandonment. Even when the actual threat of abandonment is in no way present, we continue to harbor the same old fears.

BEING EMPATHETIC TO the stories and struggles of others is one key to slowing down our selective brain functions, helping us to be aware of things we might not normally notice. Empathy lets us get out of our own heads and get the distance we need to embrace new perspectives that might (with any luck) momentarily eclipse our own. Incorporating several different viewpoints is an essential step toward deepening our creative fluency.

TRUE IMPROVISATION OR BRILLIANT RECALL

Branford Marsalis is a legendary jazz saxophonist. A jazz player's entire career is based on the ability to improvise; that is, to create new music on the spot. Under the pressure of a live performance, a skilled jazz musician can create and play spontaneous melodies over complicated chord changes, which sometimes come at break-neck speed, depending on the song's tempo. The wonder of this ability is that a master jazz soloist can create these original melodic phrases so quickly, and in such a seemingly effortless manner. When asked how many times he had actually improvised totally new jazz solos, Branford Marsalis was transparent enough to say, "Maybe three or four times in my entire career." If Mr. Marsalis wasn't creating these new pieces all the hundreds of other times he was onstage, what was he doing? His improvisations sure sound new to the rest of us.

In fact, he was drawing upon the vast canon of ideas in his musical arsenal—his memorized hard drive—and combining them in novel ways. These consist of phrases of music he'd heard or written or somehow absorbed over the course of his life. The astounding brilliance with which he puts them together is awe-some to behold. But I was floored by his honest admission that he'd actually created music spontaneously (which is axiomatic to jazz) only three or four times.

What is it about those moments when he was actually improvising that makes them so rare? I suppose it's that they were inspired, gifted, let loose from heaven and dropped into his brain. It's impossible to will that kind of inspiration, though—fruitless to look for it, to wait for it. And yet those moments are etched in his memory. My guess is that you've also had some deeply inspired moments and that you've also tried to re-create them, going over those same themes in whatever it is you do, in hopes that you'll be able to generate a similar inspiration.

Waiting for inspiration assures you only of the fact that you will most likely wait forever. The genius of Branford Marsalis and people like him isn't that he's constantly unearthing these nuggets of inspired soul gems; it's that he does the hard work of assimilating, storing, and then spitting back the tens of thousands of things he's heard, felt, or seen that have left him inspired.

TOTALLY LEGAL INSPIRING THIEVERY 101

You need to forget about what you can't control and start implementing some ideas you can control. This business of creativity is messy. You need to get your hands dirty. Let me introduce you to Totally Legal Inspiring Thievery 101. It's all about borrowing and amalgamating. Don't worry, there's nothing wrong with it. Just as an example, I'm going to take out today's *New York Times* and we're going to see if we can find some surprisingly good titles for songs. It's a fun exercise and it's guaranteed to generate some creative juices.

You may remember the story about how John Lennon came up with the title to his famous song "Happiness Is a Warm Gun." He got it from an ad in a gun magazine that producer George Martin once showed him. That's what creative and fearless people do. They borrow from everywhere and find inspiration in the least likely places. It's how Branford Marsalis got many of the licks in his musical library. He borrowed them, he aggregated them, he repurposed them, he might even have gotten them from the songs of birds; it doesn't really matter.

I'll read some headlines and pull out interesting titles and ideas for songs.

Here's the first headline I see: QATAR WIELDS OUTSIZE INFLUENCE IN ARAB POLITICS. How much do you want to bet that I can cull a powerful song title from this? Here's one:

Outsize Influence

Another headline: MAJOR CHANGES IN HEALTH CARE LIKELY TO LAST. And this song title is . . .

Likely to Last

Here's one more: JUSTICES TO HEAR HEALTH CARE CASE AS RACE HEATS UP. And this title is . . .

The Race Heats Up

I didn't even get to the body of these stories, in which there are hundreds of good titles and thought-provoking ideas buried away. This little exercise is just a microcosmic example of what I'm talking about. Open up a magazine, a Bible, or your favorite novel and drink in the thoughts and inspiration of other writers. Go to an art museum and look at one or two works that move you. To refresh your own work, no matter what your work is, use bits and pieces of what other artists, businesspeople, and teachers have done. Get away from your own voice and your own rhythm for a time. We've all inadvertently carved some deep furrows by trying to recapture those moments of our own inspiration. Now it's time to let a new rain come and erase them, making a field fresh for planting something unexpected.

Brain Bottle Opener 13: Select Your Attention/ Seeking Song Titles

With the help of colleagues at Emory University, neuroscientist Wendy Hasenkamp began testing which brain areas were related to extreme focus. She asked participants to concentrate only on their breath as their brains were scanned. They were asked to press a button at exactly the point they realized their focus had been straying from their breath. They would then resume focusing on breathing. MRI data was collected that showed which brain regions were active before, during, and after pressing the button.

Her study, published in the journal *NeuroImage*, revealed that during periods of mind wandering, regions of the brain's "default mode network," as Hasenkamp describes it, were activated. When participants became aware that their minds had drifted away from their breathing, brain regions related to useful events and ideas suddenly became active. Dr. Hasenkamp and her team found that understanding the way the brain vacillates between focus and wandering states has important implications for a number of tasks. If, for example, your mind tends to wander during an important conversation, it would be helpful if you could catch yourself as you were slipping into default mode.

By observing yourself moving away from focus, with time and training you can deliberately bring yourself back to the moment. According to Hasenkamp, this ability not only improves working memory and creative intelligence, but can even help with standardized test scores.

Right now you're going to be very selective about where you place your focus. But as opposed to the fear-based selective attention issues I've mentioned, you're going to do this without any anxiety whatsoever. Wherever you find yourself at this very moment, mentally strip away everything around you except for one tiny detail.

For example, I'm currently in my kitchen typing. Though there are literally thousands of objects, colors, smells, and sounds around me, I'm selecting only the one thing I want to focus on. *I will remove everything from my attention except for a tiny shadow on the table that's being created by the edge of a cereal box in front of me.*

For **one full minute**, see if you can draw your attention exclusively to the one detail you've chosen. Try this two or three times with different things.

In your heightened state of awareness, you can now create like John Lennon, by giving yourself **three minutes** to find as many interesting-sounding song titles as you can from the pages of a newspaper, magazine, novel, or Bible. I've even tried this with the list of ingredients on the side of a cereal box.

REAL-WORLD APPLICATIONS

Like the From Chaos to Kid-Thinking BBO and the Walk-Away
BBO, this one is something you can use to overcome rigid thinking. For example, if you are a photographer and you need new
ways to drum up business (especially since so many people think
that owning a smartphone makes them a photographer these
days), you might want to try the Select Your Attention/Seeking
Song Titles BBO to get your mind turning in ways it seldom does.
This is yet another great way to create novelty in your thought
process.

CHAPTER 14

FINDING YOUR MOTIVATION

HOW OUTCOME-CENTERED AND IMMERSIVE REWARDS WORK TOGETHER TO BRING YOUR IDEAS TO LIFE

Within each of us is a powerful engine of motivation, one that doesn't require applause, trophies, plaques, or blue ribbons. In fact, it doesn't require approval or validation of any kind. That's because this particular type of motivation comes from our joy in being totally immersed in the things we're passionate about. We are being motivated from the inside; as such, we remain independent of outside influences. I call this internal motivation "immersive motivation." But if this kind of motivation is truly internal, why, then, do we have so much trouble accessing it? Why do we constantly need to rely on external or outcome-centered motivators, like the applause or the blue ribbons I just mentioned? What blocks our access to immersive motivation is the static of negative thought constantly running through our minds.

The very notion of motivation is itself a bit of a balancing act, as you'll soon see. And in that sense, it's perfectly natural to shift between immersive motivation (which is something of an ideal) and outcome-centered motivation when undertaking a challenging goal. One of the most effective ways to attain the superiority—dare I say the purity—of immersive motivation is to underpin the ideas you're serious about bringing to life with a rock-solid structure.

For some people the word *structure* might seem counterintuitive, as if it were an inhibitor rather than a generator of creative ideas. The popular adage "There's freedom in structure" can sound paradoxical as well, when we're wrestling with a creative challenge. Just as an example, let's take a look at the eighty-eight keys on a piano. At first glance that very limited number of keys might look more like a prison than a springboard into infinite musical possibilities. How can just eighty-eight keys become a conduit to endless expression? The fact is that the limits of the piano itself become the vehicle through which a masterful pianist is able to depict a multitude of sounds and emotions. If there were an infinite number of keys, the piano would be impossible to play. It's vital to have well-defined structures in place so that your goals don't just become nebulous thoughts without anything concrete to bind them to reality. To tap into the power of immersive motivation, we need to become highly structured and highly technical. Without deep and logical structures in place Marv becomes worried. "How's this idea gonna work?" he asks, and rightly so.

When you look at the things in your life that give you the greatest sense of freedom, they are likely to be your own expressions of creativity, the most meaningful of which can leave you so inspired that you're no longer looking over your shoulder to see where the next nugget of approval is coming from. You're also likely to find that this feeling of freedom occurs most often in the areas of your life where you've imposed the most rigorous structure on yourself. Ironic in a way, isn't it? Whether it's becoming a cardiologist, being a ballet dancer, or even losing fifteen pounds, bringing your ideas to life requires that you tap into your immersive motivation. The joy of being bound up in your goal is what ultimately gives you the capacity to tolerate one of the most demanding (and in terms of manifesting your idea, most important) activities imaginable: endless, repetitive, and totally concerted practice, all done not as some draconian punishment, of course, but in order to bring real structure to an otherwise fledgling idea. The beauty of this, though, is that once you get up and running it becomes a self-perpetuating cycle, one that moves of its own energy: The structure you create fuels your immersive motivation, your immersive motivation then fuels your capacity to work on the structure, which in turn fuels you on the path toward making your goal a reality. So go ahead, make some space on your wall for those plaques and blue ribbons!

GLIRCHVILLE:
HOME TO MONSTER REWARDS

When I was six years old I loved to draw. I was often busy making what was in my head come alive with Crayolas and paper. At the time, it was a gang of monsters I called glirches, who of course lived in Glirchville. There was something so fulfilling about creating this town of Glirchville, a special place wrested from my own imagination where I could be the mayor, the policeman, the banker, the jailer, or the robber. But then, inevitably, even as I was drawing away, the simplicity of drawing for its own sake was interrupted by a thought in the back of my mind that my pictures might win me a most coveted reward: getting noticed for their brilliance by my mom and Scotch-taped up on the refrigerator door. My outcome-centered reward was clear: draw well and receive praise. It's not to say that this kind of motivation, this praise-based impetus, is without merit. Doing something for a reward does have the ability to motivate. It's just that it's often inferior to creating without any expectations at all. One who creates solely based on outcome-centered motivation is always at the mercy of factors beyond his control. His ability to bring his ideas to life will always remain contingent on the availability of a reward. And once there's an external influence looming in our thoughts, such as a refrigerator exhibition, there's also a corresponding fear: "What if it's not good enough to go on the refrigerator?"

Positive psychologists Christopher Peterson and Martin Seligman discovered that understanding and consistently practicing our best character strengths and skill sets is integral to improving our overall well-being and happiness. Because the immersive motivation we get from drawing on our innate resources is so joyous, it also tends to draw people to us. While we long to pursue our ideas for their own sake, we are equally compelled by a fear of being separated from others. That same fear triggers a primal urge to connect and to communicate. We are communal beings, after all, hardwired to intuit that our survival, not only as a species but as individuals, depends on our ability to bond with others. Our creativity—whether it's displayed in music, art, cooking, storytelling, sports, mathematics, or the simple grace of extending kindness to strangers—is what keeps us attached to one another. Ingenuity is a survival instinct and the only thing that can rival its strength is our fear of shame. If creating something wonderful binds us to a community, creating something awful separates us from that community . . . or so we fear. And since many of our fears are rooted in issues of abandonment, it makes sense that we would be motivated to use our best skill sets to become more connected to others. We are also motivated to create in order to derive a deep sense of purpose. As world-renowned author and psychiatrist Viktor E. Frankl so aptly put it: "Everyone has their own specific vocation or mission in life; everyone must carry out a concrete assignment that demands fulfillment. Therein he cannot be replaced, nor can his life be repeated. Thus, everyone's task is unique as is his specific opportunity to implement it."

This very human need to create is a mixture of both immersive and outcome-centered motivation. We love and dance and write and sing and paint and build and pray to be reassured that we are not alone. And while we crave the positive feedback that only others can provide, we also possess a strong need to do these things for no one but ourselves. Knowing that there is this duality, this seeming split in the nature of what propels us toward our goals, is to understand an important part of the creative process itself.

Best-selling author and scholar Daniel Pink writes about this tension between what he calls intrinsic and extrinsic rewards in a study called the Candle Problem. The Candle Problem shows what happens when people are either given a conceptual challenge to be solved for its own sake, or receive rewards for finding a solution to the challenge in the shortest amount of time. The participants were split into two groups and given certain items: a candle, a box of thumbtacks, and a book of matches. They were then tasked with attaching the candle to the wall so the wax wouldn't drip on the table. (See figure 1.)

FIGURE 1.

The key to solving the problem was being able to see beyond the prism of functional fixedness, an idea that we discussed in Chapter 7. Participants had to try to look at the box as more than a holder for the tacks; they had to also be able to see it as a platform for the candle. (Figure 2.)

FIGURE 2.

The solution clearly requires Kid-Thinking.

The participants in group A were told only that they were being timed to see how fast they could come up with solutions. Group B's participants were offered monetary incentives for completing the exercise quickly. The researchers found that the rewarded group took nearly three and a half minutes longer to complete the exercise than the group that was not offered an incentive.

Pink suggests, "Rewards by their very nature tend to narrow our focus." In effect, they often create their own form of functional fixedness. The study also concluded that while rewards can be effective for routine tasks, they may stifle creativity when tasks demand flexible problem solving or conceptual thinking. Pink believes that we need to revise our approach to motivation, especially since today's jobs demand a high degree of creative thinking, as well as motivation that is based on what he calls "self-determination theory," or SDT. Pink posits that self-determined motivation often turns out to be more effective for highly creative jobs than reward-based motivation. SDT proposes that people have a built-in yearning to determine the course of their lives. And when that yearning is set free, people are happier and more creative and live richer lives.

The first group in the Candle Problem was driven by immersive motivation. There are no thoughts of outcomes, judgments, or fulfilled expectations in immersive motivation. Ideally, it's an unadulterated, almost spiritual process of allowing nascent thought to be made immediately manifest without regard to anything other than the sheer joy of creation. This is the essence of working in the HourGlass, that magical time when you're so engaged in an activity that time loses all meaning (see Chapter 8). It's no coincidence that being in the HourGlass happens so often among young children. Being in that creative space, with its freedom and possibilities, is a childlike, magical experience.

The less successful, second group in the Candle Problem was

using outcome-centered motivation. When we act upon outcome-centered motivation it means that we remain acutely aware of potential rewards even as we create. It's easy to see how holding on to those kinds of expectations might have a tendency to put a drag on our creativity.

In my own work, being overly aware of what could result with the success or failure (those two words again) of a given project has historically tended to shut down my creativity, and fast. There's a power and potency to being swept up by the wave of pure creative inspiration. Consider that wave a metaphor for immersive motivation. The trouble with depending on it is that it's very hard, if not impossible, to control when that perfect wave will occur.

The analogy is quite appropriate. A big part of the joy of surfing is the unpredictability of when that perfect swell will arise. Being in the right place, at the right moment, and in the right frame of mind to harness the wave's energy makes all the difference. Ideally when I'm performing music onstage I'll be removed in a sense from what I'm doing. It's an exquisite feeling to be singing and playing without any thought as to who's in the audience or who's paying attention. It's as if I'm surfing above the music, more an observer than a performer. Then without warning, I'll become aware of how each note is coming out, of how the music is affecting the audience. That is me switching over into an outcome-centered motivation. My mind will then seem preoccupied with whether I'm being "successful" at delivering the music, rather than being a simple conduit for the music.

The trick is in knowing that everything comes in waves. You've got to find the joy in riding them all, both the easy ones and the challenging ones. Hardest of all is finding joy in waiting for the wave itself.

A SONG UNSUNG

In 1988, just a month after my wedding, my wife joined me and my band on a tour of Central Asia, which my manager at the time had set up. Island, my record company, and its president and my friend, the late Lou Maglia, instead desperately wanted me to play places like Cleveland so I could promote my record. I chose Uzbekistan, of course, but that's me.

It was there that my wife and I met an ethnomusicologist who had spent the past several years studying a remote East African tribe. He'd been observing a ritual of theirs that involved music and singing. When the tribal elders asked him to join in, he told them he didn't sing. Nothing too odd about that. "I don't sing" is something you hear people say all the time, and its meaning is straightforward; they simply don't sing. But in the case of this particular tribe, the idea that someone didn't sing was literally beyond comprehension. There wasn't a language issue. The musicologist was quite conversant in the dialect of Swahili that the tribe spoke. It was the meaning behind the words that wasn't comprehensible. For this tribe, singing was not a choice. It would be akin to saying that you don't breathe or that your blood doesn't flow. It's a very westernized sentiment that relegates creativity or a creative expression such as singing to something tangential to or somehow outside the range of normal human interaction. Singing occurs in our culture, of course, but only at specialized times and in certain environments. Someone doing a rendition of "This Land Is Your Land" or "In-A-Gadda-Da-Vida" in a typical workplace would be considered mentally unbalanced. On the flip side, it would have seemed equally strange for a member of that tribe to be either motivated by compliments or dissuaded by fear of doing something as simple and natural as singing.

Here's someone whose fear actually did keep her from singing, at least for a while. Meet Nancy Peters:

Nancy is a lovely and intelligent woman. She's a mother and a civil engineer, and she's also someone you'd go to if you needed some wise, objective advice. She is by her own admission a "good girl." She's always played it straight, got excellent grades in school, and helped with the dishes.

Yet Nancy describes herself as decidedly not creative. Being creative was a role that her older sister took on, leaving Nancy to be the capable and dependable one. "I've always wanted to sing," she tells me, "but I'm terrified at the idea of singing in front of anyone." Her dream nevertheless was to record Al Green's "Tired of Being Alone" at a professional studio and present it to her husband, Greg, on his fortieth birthday. To me this seemed like a pretty simple, straightforward idea, but from Nancy's point of view, it was anything but. So I asked her to describe herself in terms of her own creativity.

"I think I enjoy creative things. But I don't think I'm creative in the sense that I truly create. My sister Ellen is definitely the creative one in my family. She's my older sister." Nancy explained that this understanding that Ellen was the "creative one" was "established from day one. . . . Ellen is creative in all different areas; she always had this creative energy, this desire for creative output that I just lacked."

When I asked Nancy to recall something that she herself had done that she considered creative, she hesitated, finally allowing, "I would write something for school for an assignment and I'd wind up getting a great grade on it. I'd come home and they'd say, 'Yeah, nice job,' but you know, when Ellen would bring home something you could tell that there was a different kind of excitement about it. It wasn't that I hadn't done a good job or that it wasn't well written; it just didn't have that extra . . . whatever in my mind I equate with being talented or creative."

As we now know, that feeling of being less than creative is just a perception—one that's almost always proven wrong in some sense or another. I asked Nancy whether this could be true in her case. "I think for me," she said, "because my sister was three years older, she already had an advantage. I fell into being the academic one, the student, the good girl, the best helper."

It's amazing how tightly we tend to hold on to negative opinions of ourselves, regardless of whether they have real meaning. Years later, after Nancy had grown up and moved to California to start her career, she found herself in conversation with a coworker who said, "You're really funny." Nancy told me that she remembered thinking, "Wait a minute, I'm not funny. I'm not the funny one." It was one of the first times she'd realized that people were looking at her not relative to her sister, but as someone completely different from the person she'd grown up seeing in the mirror every day. It was like the baggage of her childhood had been washed away with one nice comment.

I wondered what the genesis of Nancy's idea to record a song for her husband had been. "First," she said, "you have to understand how music was in my house. It was a social activity. We would all sit around when my cousins were over, after Thanksgiving dinners, for example, and my stepfather would take out his banjo or his guitar and my uncle would pick up the other one and they would play songs and we would just hang out and sing whatever songs . . . all of us, and it didn't matter about the quality of voices. It wasn't a performance; it was more of a community. The 'performance' of singing is really scary for me."

At the time we sat down to speak, Nancy felt she wasn't anywhere near ready to begin the actual recording process. "I'm so ridiculously far behind," she said. "I can't even go there right now. I'm petrified of making a permanent record of me sounding awful. I keep thinking, 'You're gonna be so disappointed, you'll never sing again.'"

When I asked Nancy where she thought the fearful voice in her head came from she said, "It's my mom's voice and I think my mom is my biggest advocate in some ways, but she's also my biggest critic. If my mom didn't like my singing, or somehow criticized a recording I'd made, it would kill my joy. I'd probably stop singing altogether."

Nancy seemed to turn inward at this point. "Maybe it all goes back to love. Maybe it's as basic as that. When I get nice feedback I feel loved and secure, and when I don't, I feel very insecure and unloved. But one thing that's becoming abundantly clear right now is how much this whole issue of not being able to sing in front of people is something that exists only in my head. I think I can control the fear. . . . At least, I think I can control it long enough to record one song for Greg."

Nancy procrastinated for a long time, but then, with less than a week to go before her husband's birthday, she took the specific, present, and true steps that allowed her to finally book that studio time. The strong outcome-centered motivation she got from just a single encouraging phone call with the in-house recording engineer gave her the impetus to record a soulful version of "Tired of Being Alone." And by coming to understand that it was her negative thoughts alone that were crushing her innate love of singing, Nancy was able to use her rediscovered passion to harness the power of her immersive motivation as well.

Not only was Greg thrilled (thrilled to tears, I'm told) but

Nancy has rewritten the script of her life. In her words: "I'm one hundred percent more comfortable seeing myself not as the greatest talent in the world, of course, but as someone who can now freely express herself on a creative level. That's huge for me."

Brain Bottle Opener 14: Coming Back

This next Brain Bottle Opener is something I've been doing almost every day since I was fifteen. Think of it as a powerful tool that will put you almost instantly in control of your generalized anxiety. And when you seize control of your anxiety, your chances of experiencing the more effective immersive motivation increase exponentially.

First you'll need to select a short random phrase—something like "green apples are sour" or "mice walk quickly." Choose any arbitrary combination of words, of about that length; the phrase you choose is entirely up to you. Some people find it helpful to choose a phrase that comforts or encourages them.

Next, make sure you're in a place where you feel totally comfortable and sit in a chair, placing your hands gently on your thighs. Slowly breathe in through your nose and out through your mouth as if blowing through a straw with your pursed lips. Be aware of your breath as it fills your diaphragm and exits slowly as you exhale. (You should notice your stomach rising and falling with each breath.) Do this for **one minute**.

Now, instead of just breathing out, replace your exhalations with your selected phrase by drawing out each syllable for as long as your breath will allow. Remember: In through your nose, out through pursed lips. The slower the better. Be sure to make each syllable in the phrase—*Green Apples Are Sour*—a single exhalation.

Greeeeeeeeeen . . . Aaaaaaaaaa . . . ppppppppppples . . . Aaaaaaaaaarrrrrrrrrrre . . . Sooooooooooourrrrrrrrrrrr. . . .

Repeat this for **five minutes**. You *will* forget all about your phrase. Don't worry when you do. When you become aware that you've forgotten, simply come back to repeating it. If it feels good, try it for seven minutes, building up to ten after a few days.

If this BBO sounds suspiciously like meditation, you're right. (But shh, don't tell the others!) Because so many people have a bias against meditation, believing perhaps that it's too complicated or just too weird, I've given it a new name and simplified it so that it can be learned in sixty seconds.

What does it achieve? In addition to the health benefits of lowering stress, it will, as I've mentioned, open you up to creative possibilities. With this BBO in your bag of tricks, you'll have the knowledge that you can take effective, immediate control of emotions that are spinning out of control.

According to Charles L. Raison, MD, of the School of Human Ecology, at the University of Wisconsin–Madison, regular meditators have in common "a narrowing of focus that shuts out the external world and usually a stilling of the body." Dr. Raison conducted a study that showed how meditation improves both physical and emotional responses to stress. In the study, people who meditated regularly for six weeks showed "less activation of their immune systems." This means that the meditators in the study were relaxed to a degree that their immune systems didn't have to work as hard to fight off disease as the average nonmeditator. Dr. Raison also found that regular meditators showed less emotional distress when they were put in a stressful situation. For those of you still wondering what practical benefits accrue from meditating, here's an interesting one:

Munishri Ajitchandra Sagarji, a young Indian monk, has an uncanny ability for memorization. Recently, at the Sardar Vallabh-bhai Patel Stadium, in Mumbai, he dazzled a crowd of six thousand. The exhibition was part of a campaign to encourage schoolchildren to use meditation to develop mental ability, as monks have done for centuries in India. From early morning until midafternoon, audience members came to him on the stage, one at a time, to present the young monk with a random object, a complex math problem, or a word or phrase in one of six different languages. There were five hundred such items to be memorized. Munishri sat quietly meditating, absorbing everything that was told to him as note keepers in the crowd recorded each of the items. Later in the day, as the sun began to set, the monk opened his eyes and calmly recalled all five hundred. He listed each of them in perfect order and, needless to say, the crowd went wild.

REAL-WORLD APPLICATIONS

This BBO is perfect for calming an anxious mind. For example, let's say you're a law student and you're about to take the bar exam. There's no question you're going to be anxious; the test determines so much about where you'll wind up in the near future. Doing the Coming Back BBO the night before the test or, if you have time, just before the exam itself, is a perfect way to restore emotional equilibrium.

PART FOUR REVIEW

IN PART THREE you learned some ways you can begin to actually bring your dreams into the world. But starting down any new path can lead to uncertainty, and in this latest section we explored how our minds complicate our path with last-minute obstacles. To better cope with negative thoughts en route to achieving your dreams, you have done the following:

- You've written an Acknowledgment Is Knowledge statement, in which you've taken responsibility for a painful episode of change that you had previously blamed on someone or something else. This kind of acknowledgment is like cleaning a picture window of years of accumulated dirt. You are now better equipped to see not only your past, but a new dimension of your future.
- You've written a Letting Go Letter. Doing this carefully is an important step in knowing not only what you'd like to accomplish, but what bad habits you need to address in the process of achieving your goal.

- In the Select Your Attention/Seeking Song Titles BBO you were able to focus on one small previously unnoticed detail of your environment, bypassing your normal selective process. To test yourself (and your new state of hyperawareness) you went further and selected random phrases from the newspaper for song titles. This is a means of recognizing that no matter where you are, you are surrounded by creative inspiration, and that drawing from that inspiration is a good thing. It's just a question of taking the time to look, and actually trying.

- Finally, in the Coming Back BBO you allowed your mind to wander and simultaneously maintained a consciousness about returning it to a fixed point. The benefits of this simple act far exceed how little effort it actually takes. Training your mind to come back gives you the ability to control your thoughts. It's particularly helpful in quelling anxiety. Imagine how valuable it would be if you could identify a lever in your brain that you could pull every time you wanted to relieve yourself of your nervousness and harness your own built-in reward system. That's precisely what you can do with this new skill. The very knowledge of having this tool is powerful in itself.

I want you to think about how these new tools you've acquired can be applied to virtually any creative goal you set for yourself and to consider the types of circumstances when they might prove invaluable. Are you starting out on a project or are you partway down the path? Are you caught in the middle of an internal logjam, or have you been so swamped with work that you haven't had the time or clarity to focus on any one meaningful idea?

You now have an assortment of tools you can apply to a variety of circumstances that you have become better equipped to recognize, tools that you can use immediately, to make whatever it is you want start appearing bit by bit in the here and now.

You are ready to explore ways to support your dream and sustain your momentum. You'll need these final tools because no matter how much momentum you think you have, Marv is always there, always ready with his Deflators to try some new tactic to slam on the brakes.

PART FIVE

THE NURTURE

A dream doesn't die because it has no truth. It dies because you fail to nurture it.

-Susie Clevenger

CHAPTER 15

PULLING THE PLUG

STOP OVERINDULGING IN NEGATIVITY

In these final three chapters you're going to read about a few ideas that I liken to settings on some hypothetical Milky Way GPS, ideas that will help you nurture your own idea and stay on course as you get under way. But first, let me introduce you to Bonnie Rohm.

Bonnie is a naturally thin person. On her wedding day she weighed just 114 pounds, but after a pregnancy and the onset of menopause she put on so much weight she could hardly recognize herself. Always a woman of action and a self-proclaimed risk taker, Bonnie not only longed for her former thin self, she created a plan and a clear set of techniques to get thin again. That plan was key to her losing fifty pounds and keeping it off for three years and counting.

I'm always interested in people's original impetus for taking action on their ideas, and Bonnie's goal of losing weight was no different. I asked her how it began.

"Well, basically," she said, "I was always skinny. I could feel the skinny person inside that extra fifty pounds of fat. One day I came to this realization: I don't want to be this fat girl anymore." Bonnie had tried Weight Watchers and it didn't work. I was surprised to learn that she wasn't depressed at all after she was through with it. I asked her what is it that keeps her so ebullient. "For one," she said, "I'm a natural risk taker. I think everyone grows up in some sort of dysfunctional family, but mine was beyond the pale. My parents were busy growing up themselves and experiencing their own life. They left me to my own devices in many ways. I guess that neglect made me more independent."

Rather than view her painful childhood experiences as entirely negative, Bonnie was able to reframe her past as something positive. Using certain visual, textual, and imaginative points of reference, she's been able to stay focused on her goal. Here's one she's put to use: "What I would do," she said, "is picture two women: The first one has the most fabulous body, and the second is the fattest, lardiest, lumpiest lady ever. Contrasting those two images made it easier to say, 'Hey, Bonnie, we're not going in that direction. Sorry.'"

Bonnie also worked to internalize this positive approach: "Lately, I try and listen and appreciate when someone says thank you to me for something that I did, or when someone tells me, 'You look good.' I really try and accept that, because it's those messages I want to put back in my head. Learning to love yourself is difficult—really difficult—but it's so important."

THIS AD BROUGHT TO YOU BY MAJORLY AFRAID OF REVEALING VULNERABILITY INC.

Dr. David Fischman is an acclaimed author and a civil engineer. He's penned five books, including *The Secret of the Seven Seeds: A Parable of Leadership and Life.* Among the many important statistics he presents is this: By age ten the average child in the Western world will have seen more than one million advertisements. The nation of Denmark, Dr. Fischman writes, was rated in a recent study as the Western country with the happiest people. Interestingly, it also happens to be the country with the least amount of advertising. Our inability to disconnect from advertising and the media overall can often leave us feeling so empty as to have forgotten what compels us, what it is that drives us to engage with the world. Transfixed by the digital glow, we remain convinced we are somehow less than the woman with the perfect breasts and shiny hair, less than the man with the BMW, and less than the family with the straight white teeth and the biggest house on the block.

The more time we spend glued to our entertainment screens the more time we spend imbibing ideas about our own insufficiency. Methodical disconnection from technology is as imperative as our healthy integration with technology, particularly since we are only standing at the very threshold of technology's advance.

I have a personal relationship with the idea of leaving technology of all kinds behind on a regular basis; I observe the Jewish Sabbath, a time when the use of technology is prohibited. And while I don't believe that the strict tenets of this observance are appropriate for most people, I am strongly convinced that many of its main ideas would be helpful if they were incorporated on some level. Technically speaking, there are thirty-nine types of labor that are prohibited on the Sabbath. They include things like using money, making fire, planting, carrying things from a public to a private domain, sewing, cooking, fastening two things together, and writing. Over time, each of the thirty-nine prohibitions was extrapolated on to prohibit the use of things that weren't in existence at the time these laws were created.

Some examples are driving a car, which runs on a combustion engine and is a violation of the prohibition against the use of fire; and using electronics of any sort, which demands a completed circuit and is a violation of the principle of joining two things together. This last prohibition effectively renders all cell phones, computers, and televisions completely off-limits during the twenty-five hours of the Sabbath.

I was recently involved in a creativity symposium in San Francisco. Among the speakers was Bill Wasik, former senior editor at *Wired* magazine. Before the event, Bill and I had a chance to speak about the idea of stepping back from technology, and how the rituals of Shabbat echoed a very important, if often missing, dimension of technology itself: our ability to shut it off. Not just to shut it off once a year, or for a few moments throughout a day, but by a regular, systematized means. Bill observed that this ritual pointed not to some ancient and irrelevant past, but to a decidedly post-modern view of our integration with technology.

DURING MY WORKSHOPS I almost always have participants write the Smartphone Letter (Brain Bottle Opener 5). As recently as two years ago, I had to ask that people bring their phones to the workshops. Today, that suggestion is as absurd as asking them to bring their livers. And while I strongly believe that as a tool, it is perhaps the most miraculous thing ever created on the planet, I'm also cognizant of the smartphone having made us into actual cyborgs, human beings whose abilities have been enhanced by technology. The very real danger is that as we progress deeper and deeper into the offerings of technology, many of us—perhaps most of us—will be completely cut off to the experience of ever living without the technology.

What's the problem, you ask, with using the cyborg "advantage" in the first place? A host of reasons come to mind: losing touch with simple human experiences such as conversation, solitude, reflection, intimacy, and feeling the awesomeness of nature. But mostly, it involves the cost. I'm not talking about the purchase price of our devices. I'm talking about the fact that every communication-related technology seems to also be a platform and driver of advertising, and nearly every ad tells us that we are not good enough. With a steady diet of messaging that exists to explain how we're not complete people unless we do or buy or become X, it's no wonder we've lost touch with our creative spirit.

Each time we use a search engine, listen to Spotify, or watch a video on YouTube, we are being sold something, and 99.999 percent of the time, it's nothing we need or even want. Marketers are watching us through our every keystroke and gaining a keener understanding not only of what we aspire toward but also, ominously, what we fear.

Taking time away from ideas and influences that tell us only about our shortcomings is partly how we avoid becoming Stuck-Thinkers. Doing so requires a strategy, a methodology to counter the sway of the multibillion-dollar industries, which exist in part to disable us, to mollify and flatten us, so that in the end, we become susceptible to whatever advertisers want to sell us.

I'm by no means a Luddite or a conspiracy theorist. I'm just aware that there are natural economic forces that work by their own rules and contain their own power—power we must endeavor to understand if we want to manifest our personal dreams. We will be better prepared to understand this power and how we can effectively integrate it into our lives if we can find ways to disconnect from technology on a regular basis.

The work comes primarily from becoming mindful about technology's encroachment into your own life and the lives of your family and friends. To be mindful requires that you step back, draw a deep breath, and then take an objective look at where you stand in relation to this ever-expanding force in your life.

Brain Bottle Opener 15: Disconnect to Reconnect

Allow **two minutes** to pick one day this week for a four-hour technological fast (not including times when you'd normally be asleep). During this four-hour digital/technological fast you will not use:

telephone or smartphone
electric lights
e-mail
computer
radio
record player
car
cigarette lighter
amplified instrument
camera
microwave oven
electric can opener . . .

In short, pretty much any technology that was invented after the mid-1700s. See how four hours feels. If it's too much, reduce the time. If it feels like you can do more, go for it. The trick is to make this a regular part of your weekly rhythm, to get this technological fast as fully integrated into your life as possible so that there's more time for things that don't cost much: meals together, love, communication, bonding—real memory creation with the people you're closest to.

REAL-WORLD APPLICATIONS

This BBO isn't an exercise per se; it's a way of life. Imagine you're an elementary school teacher and you're tasked with having to create a new lesson plan every evening for your next day's class. Doing this BBO at least once a week will give you a window into the many creative ideas latent in your mind. These thoughts may well have been inspired by things you've seen on TV or on the Internet. I'm not saying our new technologies aren't a fantastic source for creativity. But going on regular technological fasts will give you a chance to assimilate and incorporate your ideas. You can't have information feeding in constantly. In order to generate ideas, the stream of information intake ultimately needs to be suspended. Allowing space in your mind for new and proactive ideas to take root has the added benefit of combating negative thinking. Your negative assumptions will no longer have free rein; they'll have to compete with your positive thoughts, for a change! A particularly good time to do this BBO is when you feel so harried that disconnecting from technology feels impossible. That may be a sign that it's a propitious time to do so.

CHAPTER 16

OF POSSES AND PUZZLES

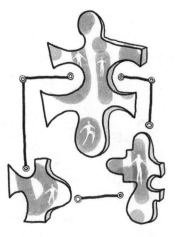

HOW A SUPPORT SYSTEM CAN MAKE THE DIFFERENCE BETWEEN A DREAM PURSUED AND A DREAM ABANDONED

Your posse is a collective of any size (it could be just one other person) that can serve as a sounding board, a guardrail, or a cheerleading section to keep your dream on track. It's particularly helpful when your enthusiasm for your goal is waning. Surrounding yourself with supportive people is key, and if you don't already have a group of friends you can call on to form your posse, you can get started in almost any city in the world by searching the Internet. If you like to knit, you can find a knitting group nearby. You can find classical music groups, writer's workshops, woodworking groups, skydiving communities, and filmmaking collectives. Creative people are clamoring to meet other people with similar interests and synergize their ideas. While the idea of having someone in your corner is hardly new, I find that in nearly every case in which a person finds the challenge of bringing her ideas to life to be too great, she's neglected to take this simple step. There are no cases that I've ever seen in which someone was able to fully develop her ideas without some sort of help from another person.

A PUZZLE SOLVED

The last person we're going to hear from is Debbie Gold, an exceptionally fearless innovator and someone who benefited enormously from the feedback and support she received from her posse. Debbie was a tour manager with rock acts ranging from the Grateful Dead to Bob Dylan. After years of work on the road she created a job for herself that had never existed. She became the first person to act as an agent not for rock acts themselves, but for sound engineers and producers. I met her when I was working with my good friend, the late producer/engineer Don Smith, who was responsible for hits with acts like Tom Petty, U2, and the Rolling Stones.

As the music business continued to fall into its current state of disruption, Debbie knew that she had to reinvent herself yet again. She came up with something totally unexpected, but still within the range of her specialized skill set. Her idea was simple, definitely of the why-didn't-I-think-of-that variety. (Well, we didn't and she did.) She created a best-selling line of jigsaw puzzles using LP covers of famous music acts—Jimi Hendrix, Johnny Cash, the Grateful Dead, and others—called RedisCover Jigsaw Puzzles. It was an elegant and simple idea.

Just as Debbie unearthed the hidden value of seemingly useless and outmoded objects such as vinyl LP covers, she found the hidden value in her own experiences and her many supporters. One person in particular helped with encouragement, ideas, and constructive critiques along the path to making Debbie's goals become reality. Sure, Debbie's idea was simple, but think about how painstaking it must have been for her to see the idea through to the finish. Licensing agreements, intellectual property rights issues, dealing with estates, lawyers . . . you name it. Here's how she did it and how her posse was integral to her success:

To Debbie, it seemed so unusual that she'd come up with a puzzle. That was about the last thing she ever thought she'd do, but as she looked back at all the different things she'd done in her career—road-managing acts, representing producers, putting bands together like a casting agent, and all the novel things she did over the years—it started to make sense. In her words, "I'm an idea person." I asked Debbie what she felt being an idea person entails. "I've done things that have literally never been done before," she said. "I knew that David Geffen was looking for a producer for a band of his. I just made it happen and then I realized, 'Wait a minute, I think this is a great idea, to have producers be represented by an agent.' It was the first time it was ever done and then people chased after me to do it for them. I literally made that up. The point of this is that you have to be brave."

Experience has taught us all that there's always somebody who's going to haul off and criticize a novel idea, and I wondered what Debbie's particular strategies were for dealing with the naysayers—how did she cope with the emotional blows? "First off," she told me, "you always run the risk of somebody not taking you seriously or not listening to you, so I think it's really about following your instincts and knowing that you can have a voice. When I'm afraid I often think, 'If this is so good, why hasn't anybody done it before?'"

How many of us also come up with great ideas like Debbie's, perhaps as we're lying in bed, ideas that we totally dismiss by the time we're dressed and out the door in the morning? One of the ways Debbie was able to sustain her idea was using the impetus she got from her posse when she brought her nascent puzzle concept to her friend Bob Weir, the guitarist for the Grateful Dead. After getting great initial feedback from him, she would meet with Weir periodically to talk through her ideas as they continued to develop.

Weir gave her the support she needed, along with clear strategies to bring her idea to fruition. She told me, "The day I actually held the first finished puzzle in my hand was magical. It gave me a profound sense of the power of my own imagination."

I know that Debbie is well aware that from time to time we all get notions about the way we'd like things to be. But she also knows that most people can't follow through on those fleeting visions. As we concluded our discussion, she put down the puzzle pieces she'd been holding and thought for a moment before saying, "I think the act of following through is a lot about undoing the negativity we've learned over the years. When you're a little kid, you believe you're smart and that you have great instincts. You do creative things like talk to invisible people; you believe in all kinds of stuff. Then you're taught, 'Oh, grow up. Don't be immature.

Don't be this, don't be that.' I think that you have to unlearn some of this. It's mostly about trusting yourself and then surrounding yourself with trusted people who can support your ideas."

FORM YOUR PERSONAL POSSE

Just after I lost my job on *Bones*, I began meeting with my own personal posse to help get over feeling like the biggest loser in the world. This posse consists of about ten trusted friends, all successful people, who often feel that their best creative years are behind them. To say aloud that you feel a little lost or a little old or a little worthless is hard for people to do. We need our spouses, our friends, our kids, our clients, our parents, and our bosses to keep on believin' that we've got everything under control.

Oftentimes we get so good at purveying the control myth that we start believing our own fiction, and of course, that's precisely where the trouble starts. To protect ourselves we begin by deluding the people around us, and then without noticing, we begin to delude ourselves. At that point we've become so lost we don't even know we're lost. My posse provides enormous help to those of us who feel a little marginalized, a little left behind in a world in which being over thirty is something to be worn like a scarlet letter. We serve as one another's personal board members, listening, mostly, giving some advice, and listening some more. I know it sounds a bit odd and maybe even indulgent to say this, given all the trouble facing the world, but the struggles we have are far from small. We've all got families to support, people who depend on us to keep our confidence up and our creative juices flowing. The posse is how we help to keep each other in the very condition most of us never thought we'd be in again: highly energized, impassioned, and inspired.

The other thing we do is encourage one another to take risks. Simple things, such as learning to dance, in my case. My wife and, to be fair, many others, have remarked that I am literally the worst dancer they've ever seen. In spite of that, I took a tango class recently, and for the first time, I saw how I could become, with a great deal of practice, something slightly less than a total embarrassment to my species. But the truth is, at my age I don't really mind looking like a fool once in a while.

Not avoiding embarrassment is the whole point. It's the way we developed our skills in the first place. No kid ever picks up a guitar or hits a speed bag or goes in for a layup perfectly the first few times. It's just that when we're young, it's expected that we won't be perfect. Somewhere along the way, after receiving a certain number of accolades, we lose touch with the beauty, the poignancy of making mistakes.

That's what the posse does best: It helps people relearn how to be comfortable with making mistakes. And through those mistakes and particularly the freedom from the fear of not appearing to be perfect, we are made joyful again. The joy comes from the renewal of possibility. When you have that, you get this wonderfully elusive and very human feeling called hope. And I ask you, is there a greater joy than having a reinvigorated sense of hope?

Here's how to get started: Call a friend and ask for advice. Everyone likes to dole it out and it's a great way to break the ice and elevate the tenor of your conversations. Start a dialogue that goes beyond talking about the weather or, worse, having a non-conversation that's merely a rehashing of that endless laundry list of complaints. Talk about rebirth; talk about getting outside yourself and doing things for other people. Talk about the things you loved and dreamed about as a kid and about real, practical ways you can start doing those things again today.

If you're still wondering why a posse is crucial for bringing your ideas to fruition, consider this: The Posse Foundation, a national organization dedicated to helping public high school students get into college, has been instrumental in giving a leg up to students lacking the resources available to wealthier families. Since 1989, these Posse scholars—many of whom are from urban centers and might have been overlooked by traditional college selection processes—have been receiving four-year, full-tuition leadership scholarships. The Posse Foundation's remarkable success rate in producing college graduates is 90 percent. In major American cities, the college graduation rate for students outside the Posse Foundation's program can be as low as 10 percent. Much of the foundation's work is done through a one-on-one mentorship program, which helps keep the students inspired and accountable.

EXTERNAL DEFLATORS— NEGATIVITY FROM WITHOUT

While it's true that posses are essential for helping you bring your ideas into the world, you need to be careful about who you share your goals with, especially in the early stages. Because they're still underdeveloped, these nascent ideas are fragile like gossamer, and especially susceptible to discouragement. Marv is ready to pounce on them, for sure, and if someone from the outside gets in there and digs a hole into your early-stage dream, Marv might just be able to finish it off. Here's a letter a fan wrote to me with this very problem:

> Peter, I've recently finished an early draft of a book of poetry and though I've been excited and confident about it for the most part, I've found my enthusiasm waned dramatically after showing it to a friend and getting a lukewarm response. Laura H.

My response:

> Dear Laura,
> I really wish I could have shared what I'm going to say to you before you let your friend read the manuscript. But since you already have, consider it as my Grandma Rose used to say in Yiddish, "b'sheret"—meant to be.
> Here's the cold truth about friendships: Oftentimes people whom we consider to be our good friends may be harshly critical of things we are passionate about. I call these people External Deflators (or EDs). EDs' negative tendencies (just like Marv's team of internal Deflators) make ideas that haven't had a chance to fully form extremely susceptible to negative feedback. EDs are functionally fixed and as such they're bringing Stuck-Thinking to the table when they should be bringing Kid-Thinking.
> I think of my own work in its early stages as tender shoots that can be easily uprooted and destroyed. Knowing this, I'm always very judicious about who I'll let see early drafts of things I create. I'm not looking for people to fawn over the ideas at this early stage, but I am looking for

guidance and support. As such, I'm selective in presenting these early iterations only to people who are familiar with the process of inventing things, people who through their own experience with innovation are knowledgeable and sensitive about the delicate nature of early work.

I'm not only lucky to have such people in my life, I've actively sought them out over the years as kindred spirits and I've cultivated friendships based on the knowledge that we offer one another support, inspiration, and guidance as opposed to so-called "constructive criticism," which in many cases feels like a thinly veiled means of throwing cold water on a project.

I'm not a cynic. I believe most people's motives are good. It's just that EDs are not empathetic, so they fail to realize the damage they're causing. They don't try to problem solve (what an innovator does); they problem-identify and think the idea lacks merit because of the problem's existence. All creation is a process of creating order and solutions out of chaos and problems. It's a process of motion—going from one place to another. Saying something is bad completely disregards how close to great it might actually be.

So, Laura, it's impossible for me to determine just how your friend's comments are intended and what your level of sensitivity to the comments might actually be, though my suspicion is aroused whenever I see someone go away "deflated" as opposed to strengthened after an encounter. The questions to ask yourself are these: Were you uplifted by the conversation with your friend (even if it included advice and opinions that might differ from your own), or were you made to feel humiliated and that your aspirations had no merit? It's vital that you take your creative ideas into the world. Yet, you must always exercise the appropriate caution in not bringing things that are still in process to an External Deflator.

Brain Bottle Opener 16: Support List

First take **two minutes** to create a list of people you feel will be supportive in your quest to make your dream real. Then take another **five minutes** to e-mail at least one of those people to schedule a time to meet. Be prepared to ask to meet with that person either face-to-face or by phone at least three times in the next ninety days.

Remember, the purpose of your posse is to provide reaffirming support as you unleash your Big Muse, but it's surprising how many people forget this important step. At a minimum, that person from your list is your support team. He or she is not the manager of your dreams or your gatekeeper. You alone must provide the overall direction. Incidentally, if you can't think of anyone who can serve as your posse member, use the time in this BBO to make a list of local workshops, collectives, and interest groups that you can call on to develop your posse and work from there.

Finally, keep your list of names (or the workshop resources) and your meeting schedule on a wall where you can see it every day.

If for some reason you find yourself feeling like you need a bigger posse before you can move forward, that's Marv talking. One good human being is all you'll need.

REAL-WORLD APPLICATIONS

Let's say you're switching careers; for instance, going from stock market trader to certified financial planner. Even though they are related fields, there are challenging certification exams to be taken (and passed), new skills to be mastered, and a new crop of clients to be found. The differences between these two jobs are apparent enough to create a great deal of anxiety. Having a list of friends, colleagues, or teachers whom you know for certain you can call upon to discuss your apprehensions and ideas can be a powerful motivator as you move forward. Having a concrete schedule of when you will be in touch takes this feeling of control one step further.

The list and the schedule are just paper, after all. They won't talk to you or take you out dancing, but you will feel encouraged and embraced in very real ways, by seeing the names on the list and knowing the precise times you will be in touch with your posse.

CHAPTER 17

FUSING FORM AND STRUCTURE

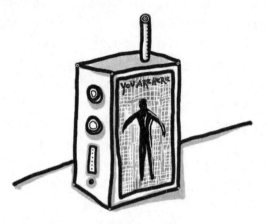

HOW TO STAY SINGING THROUGH ROUGH WEATHER

Aviation navigation is a continual process of course correction. Most people don't realize that 95 percent of the time, any given plane in the sky is being thrown off course by wind, weather, and other factors. One of the pilot's main jobs is making constant small navigational adjustments. Similarly, someone who's successfully pursuing a goal will spend much of his or her time just trying to stay on track.

Successful dream makers act like these pilots. They are comfortable with the idea that course correction is a natural part of dream catching. They know that there is no such thing as a perfectly straight line connecting them from point A to point B. They also know that having strategies in place to keep their goals on track is essential for getting them where they need to go.

Throughout the book, I've outlined numerous tactics you can use, not only for getting started but also for staying on your path: lists of the people who will remain supportive, reminders about the ways your life can change for the better when you follow through on your ideas, strategies to help you disconnect from distracting people and media, even writing a letter to yourself to remind you of things you need to let go of before you can move ahead.

All the techniques we've looked at in the book create harbors of safety for when the inevitable storm winds blow and threaten to throw your dream off course.

This last Brain Bottle Opener is something I use in all my Big Muse workshops. In fact, it's the culmination of all the previous BBOs. For those of you who are already songwriters, this next bit of instruction will be one more tool to use in your creative arsenal. For those who've never written a song, this will be your chance to create a cogent, creative statement that can serve as the theme song of your personal dream. It will help to keep you focused and on point.

If you have no interest in writing a song and are perhaps saying, "I want to spend my valuable time developing my own ideas," let me be clear: I hear you. The reason I'm asking you to create a song in the first place is because it will powerfully assist you in visualizing your own particular dream, making you that much better prepared to establish it in the real world.

Engagement with music and songs on any level—writing

them, listening to them, playing them, dancing to them, and singing them—has the additional benefit of allowing information of all types to stay fresh in the mind and the memory. Dr. Henry L. Roediger III, an expert in the study of memory retrieval and a professor of psychology at the Washington University in St. Louis Memory Lab, explains: "Our brains have what amount to two hulking mainframe computers: the hippocampus and the frontal cortex." They are the two areas most associated with memory and they are capable of processing millions of bits of information daily. Dr. Roediger says that from a neurological perspective, getting information into those areas isn't the tricky part. The challenge we face is pulling that data back out. "Music," he says, "provides a rhythm and a rhyme and occasionally an alliteration in the lyric. All of this is what makes a song helpful in information retrieval."

If we were asked to recite all the words to a Beatles song, Dr. Roediger says, "We couldn't do it unless we sang it in our minds." Music is a natural cuing device, but it's the song's structure that allows a person to get at the information it holds. Music is a powerful repetition engine. It's not necessarily the song's melody, but the overall formal structure (along with the melody) that promotes the repetition, which is what promotes memorization. That's why patients in advanced stages of Alzheimer's have been known to sing along to familiar songs. Dr. Roediger also says that neuroscientists believe humans developed music and dance to aid in the retrieval of information. "The idea was that the chant would help people to remember large sets of information across the ages."

As you begin the process of writing your song, don't worry at all if you're not a musician. The most difficult part of writing a song for most people (songwriters included) is often the lyrics, which anyone can write. And that's what we're going to deal with now.

Here are the simple steps to creating your very own lyrical mission statement.

Brain Bottle Opener 17: Write Your Song

Following the instructions listed in this BBO, you will write song lyrics that contain the essence of one of your dreams.

Think of it as your own personal theme song. It will consist of three verses of four lines each. When you're done, you'll have written twelve lines.

Hang up a copy of your finished song on your refrigerator or your bathroom wall and sign your name to it following this format:

"Thirty Crates of Kale" Copyright 2016 by Susan T. Everywoman

This little detail can give you a stronger relationship to your song. Then, if you're musical, you can always write a melody for it. If not, find a guitar or piano teacher from a local music store and ask him or her to help you with a melody.

Make sure to send the lyrics or an MP3 of the song to a friend. Putting it out into the world changes you, and it just might change the world.

Are you ready to start? Think of everything we've covered so far—you can do this! Remember, tiny, specific steps.

START BY PREPARING

Gather information. Go to a quiet place and give yourself **three minutes** to concentrate on the dream you want to pursue (that dream you thought about or wrote down at the beginning of the book or listed in the Two-Minute Drill). The first step is to picture as much as you can about the physical experience of seeing your dream made manifest. Imagine yourself in the midst of pursuing your dream. Envision yourself in that place, working on that goal. Use your FutureVision to see it vividly as it comes into focus.

Make a sensory list. Now give yourself **two and a half minutes** to Kid-Think and write down the sensations you're imagining: the sights, smells, sounds, touch . . . Where are you? Precisely what are you experiencing as you go about making your dream come true? Go for the minutiae. Consider nothing too insignificant—the smaller the detail, the better. For example, someone who has a dream of becoming a photographer might visualize herself shooting a high school football practice in late fall in northern Minnesota. The list she creates might look something like this:

> Cold wind on a November afternoon, crows cawing, bonfire burning, freezing fingers, a train rumbling in the distance, the sound of young men yelling, grunting, shoulder pads and helmets colliding, cleats making rhythm on the frozen ground, an old man walking a dog, a goalpost against a steel-gray sky, an early sunset, breath coming out as steam, a muddy field.

Notice that there is no meaning associated with these images; they're simply observations and sense perceptions. Think of them as the opening to a movie that's playing in your mind. The credits are rolling, there's music and sounds, but there is no story yet, just a series of pictures. The camera pans from left to right and the images place you in the scene.

Make a list of emotional insights. The next step in gathering information is to create a list of the emotions that are associated with bringing your dream into existence. Give yourself **two and a half minutes** to jot down the feelings you get as you see your goal coming closer. How are you different? What is your emotional reaction to finally seeing your dream leave your head and manifest itself in the real world? Here are some examples of emotional insights that our hypothetical photographer might use:

> I feel awake to possibility. I can't wait to submit these pictures to the Brainerd Dispatch. I feel alive. It feels good to be here . . . as the sun is going down the pictures are becoming more dramatic. I feel engaged, hopeful . . . I want to buy the Sony a99; it's an amazing camera. I am happy to be here. I'm not worrying about anything. I can't wait to send these pictures to Dave. I'm just trying to get the images to look their best. I feel free. The world looks beautiful to me now.

A NOTE ON STRUCTURE

Next, after you've made your two lists, it's time to turn your sensory list and the emotional insights list into a song. The first thing to learn about songwriting is that, just like everything else in life, songs need a structure to stand on. There are an unlimited number of structures that you could use for your song. Some have verses that don't rhyme and some have complicated bridges and odd time signatures, but for now I want you to use one song structure in particular. The following song is something I just made up off the top of my head (so don't judge me too harshly!). I wrote it to illustrate a well-known, very simple structure, which is especially useful for first-time songwriters. More advanced songwriters will recognize it as a forcing frame that can be used to create a compact and elegant song as well. Stay with this exact structure; it's an easy-to-work-with, time-tested classic. Check out the title and the first verse:

Black-Winged Bird

1. She's gone and left me out in the cold
2. Don't know how much pain my poor heart can hold
3. She took off for Lubbock without saying a word
4. Flew outta my life like a **black-winged bird**

If you look at the preceding verse, you'll see a few obvious things. First is that the title ends with a simple word that is both evocative and easy to rhyme with: *bird* (word, heard, third, blurred, curd, stirred, nerd, absurd . . .). Second is that the first two lines rhyme with each other, as do the last two. The final thing to be aware of is that in this particular song structure the fourth line always ends with the title—in this case, "Black-Winged Bird."

SONGWRITING STEPS

1. **Choose a title.** First take **one minute** to choose a title from either your sensory list or your emotional insights list. Look for something that appeals to you, but make sure it's easy to rhyme with. In this particular song structure, you don't want to use a title like "The Garrulous Crustacean Antecedents." It's going to be too hard to find rhymes for a title like that (though it might make a cool band name). I'm going to choose a line to use as a title directly from my hypothetical photographer's sensory list: Cleats making rhythm on the frozen ground. I'll shorten it to: "Rhythm on Frozen Ground."

    I didn't spend too much time deciding on that title. I just liked the sound of it, and the word *ground* rhymes easily. Now, before you actually start writing (or running for the hills), let's walk through the process of creating each line.

2. **Create a first line.** Simply pick one of the phrases from your lists. Select it deliberately or randomly—it doesn't really matter; just pick something that moves you. I'm going to go with "cold wind on a November afternoon."

    Reading back that phrase, I can see in my mind's eye what that football field looks like and feels like. I take off my gloves and I can feel that wind on my fingers as I shoot the pictures. . . .

3. **Create a second line.** Compose a second line that resonates with your feelings about seeing your

dream come true, or simply pick another phrase from either list. The only requirement is that it rhymes with your first line—in this example: Cold wind on a November afternoon. (And don't be afraid to use a rhyming dictionary. They're available for free all over the Internet.) How's this:

Cold wind on a November afternoon
I feel alive, my dream is coming soon.

4. **Create a third line.** Next, write a third line in that same vein, making sure that the last word of the line rhymes with the last word of the title you've chosen, which will finish your fourth line—"Rhythm on Frozen Ground," in my case.

So my finished first verse looks like this:

Cold wind on a November afternoon,
I feel alive, my dream is coming soon.
I'm capturing the world and the sun is goin' down,
As cleats make rhythm on frozen ground.

Now make one more verse of four lines using the same technique. I'll try the following lines for my second verse, still choosing many of them directly from either my sensory or my emotional list:

I'm happy to be here, not worrying 'bout a thing,
The crows caw, as my heart begins to sing.
I'm hopeful at last as I hear the sound,
Of cleats making rhythm on frozen ground.

Now let's write one more four-line verse.

I feel awake to possibility, as a bonfire's burning,
It started coming in clear, just as I started yearning.
This dream of mine's a miracle I found,
As cleats make rhythm on frozen ground.

It's time to write your three verses, each made up of four lines, with your title as the last part of your fourth line. Remember to use your sensory and emotional lists for inspiration, and stay within the set structure.

Try not to overthink, and don't worry about having to make literal or linear sense. Many of the songs we love most, be they "Strawberry Fields Forever," "Wichita Lineman," or "Tangled Up in Blue," almost never make literal sense. They do, however, all evoke strong feelings. Sacrificing literal meaning for emotional heft is often what makes a song resonate.

The title of my hypothetical photographer's song, "Rhythm on Frozen Ground," doesn't need to mean anything. The image it conveys, especially in the context of the photographer's dream, is powerful in and of itself.

Notice that the lines I've used from this song have been almost exclusively pulled from the sensory list and the list of emotional insights. Except for tweaking a few phrases to make them rhyme, it was as if the work of writing the song had already been done for me. This happened because I could see and feel myself in that hypothetical scenario up in northern Minnesota in my mind's eye. Occasionally, songwriting should and can feel effortless.

FINAL STEP: YOUR TURN

Now go to a quiet place and give yourself **ten minutes** to write and finish your song. Don't worry that it isn't enough time, because it is. You can always come back and polish it later. For now I want you to feel the urgency of the time limits I'm giving you. Trust me, the limits are a good thing. This is the moment to Kid-Think without thoughts of external reward. Look for the immersive motivator. If you feel lost, go back and review the sample song I wrote.

What I'm going to say now might sound odd but it's important: *Get comfortable with the idea of writing something that is pure crap.* Yeah, pure, unadulterated crap. Just finish it. That's the goal—the finish, not the genius. Again, be comfortable with writing something horrible. I'm serious.

There's a metaphor I use occasionally that's perfect (and you know by now, I'm fond of metaphors—I'm a songwriter, after all) but I hesitate to use it because it's, well, less than dignified. But here goes: You should treat the products of your imagination exactly as you treat your own bowel movements. They're just something that happens. No sane person is offended by or afraid of his or her own waste; that would be weird. And it's just as weird to be offended by or afraid of the products of your own imagination, whether they're brilliant or worthless. The harsh judgment is what kills the creative process.

It's just like those karate guys, the one out of three hundred I talked about in Chapter 6, who weren't afraid of getting hit. Don't let your fear of being "bad" prevent you from accomplishing the goal of simply following the form I've given you and finishing your song. This kind of unabashed Kid-Thinking will help you dive into your Milky Way Moment. Just write. If you need to use a rhyming dictionary, go for it. If you need a thesaurus, there are great ones on the Internet. Books, magazines, dictionaries—anything that helps is fair game. Think less and write more. I'll say it twice more for you: Think less, write more. Think less, write more. At some point you need to simply give way to doing. *That point is now.*

REAL-WORLD APPLICATIONS

Aside from the fact that I'm a professional songwriter, there are a couple of reasons the Write Your Song BBO is a central metaphor in my Big Muse seminars. First, songs are short. They're not screenplays, novels, or symphonies. As such, they can be created in a relatively short time. The other reason is that a song is a beautiful metaphor for creativity itself. It is by its very nature highly structured, so much so that its form can often seem constraining. Consider the song's structure analogous to left-brained thinking. On the other hand, the rigid structure needs to be filled with connective, original, utterly human and emotional thought. Think of that aspect of a song as analogous to right-brained thinking.

The extent to which you are successful in creating that emotional connectivity within your structure will determine the power of your song. In this sense, a well-crafted song is the perfect fusion of both left- and right-brained thought processes. In terms of practicality, this BBO is the mother lode. I won't even deign to list its potential applications. Suffice it to say that there is nothing you can create, no dream that you can fulfill that doesn't contain these two opposites (structure and form) in equal measure.

PART FIVE REVIEW

HERE WE ARE at the conclusion of the book. Let's take one final look at where we are and what we've covered in this last section.

- By doing the Disconnect to Reconnect BBO, you committed to a four-hour technological fast one day this week, during which you abstained from using any modern technology. The quietude of technological disconnection enables you to reconnect with your natural focus and energy. In the din and confusion of your life, it's going to be reassuring to know that you have a means of shutting down the things that distract you from achieving your dream.
- You created a posse you believe will support you on your quest to make your vision a reality. The list is just paper and ink, of course, but the names you wrote symbolize an inestimable source of encouragement. Knowing that you can call on your support system (and actually doing so) will keep you on track whenever you falter.

- And finally, you wrote the lyrics to a song—consider it your personal dream theme song. Having it handy to recite or sing will help keep your vision clear and alive.

I talked a lot about vision throughout this book, creating a picture of the way things ought to be, the way they could be. Vision doesn't come only from things we can see. The vision I'm referring to, the FutureVision, is more like an accumulation of evidence. It's a step-by-step process. At some point, probably without you ever even being aware, there will come an intuitive understanding that will lead you to know that this thing you desire, this dream of yours, is far more real than you could have ever imagined.

PUTTING IT ALL TOGETHER

LUCIDA•FUTURUM

IT'S TIME TO wrap things up. Here's a condensed look at the various ways you have now learned to let out your Big Muse. You'll recall that your Big Muse is your instinctual capacity for creativity. We're each gifted with it. Remember that when I say "creativity" I don't necessarily mean in terms of art or music, or any of the things we normally associate with the word, so don't be confused. It's your creative spirit I'm talking about, your native creative energy, and if your dream is not materializing, it's because your Big Muse is bottled up. You need to let it out, but it can't come out until your fear of embarrassment or disappointment is outweighed by your desire to see your idea made manifest. When your need to create is just that much greater than your fear, you become a Kid-Thinker.

A Kid-Thinker is able to react fearlessly, without Marv, that negative voice inside your head constantly telling you you're not good enough, not pretty enough, or not smart enough. Remember that even though Marv is annoying, his goal isn't to make your life miserable. All he's trying to do is spare you from failure, which in his paranoid thinking leads to shame, and then to abandonment. Marv has been with you forever. He was there to protect you when you were young. And when he's truly intent on "saving" you from change, he reminds you:

- If you do something stupid you will feel shame.
- Shame will lead to abandonment.
- And (*bong* . . . the bell of doom tolls) abandonment means death.

Fear is why you're afraid to express your vulnerability, and vulnerability is nothing more than openness to the challenges new ideas present. That's why vulnerability (under the appropriate circumstances) is such a big driver of the creative process.

Your FutureVision is your highly detailed image of your fulfilled life. Marv will prevent you from seeing it as long as you're not actually doing anything to make it happen. Once you start the careful process of clarifying your FutureVision, you'll have less imposition from Marv.

To prevent you from unleashing your Big Muse, Marv enlists the services of the Deflators. They're nothing more than the details of your own imagination turned against you and your dreams. The Deflators will bind you with Elephant Ropes, your painful memories, which keep you bound to a vulnerable past. When you're transfixed by these memories you become too afraid to pursue your dream. In this state you can easily become trapped by a Logjam, a depression that will leave you utterly stuck. You can break the Log-jam by writing a Letting Go Letter, which is a tool that helps you determine what you need to get rid of in your life. The Letting Go Letter examines the people, things, or beliefs you need to cut out of your life before you can move forward again. Clearing that emotional space will help reignite an extinguished FutureVision.

When Marv and his Deflators have you trapped, you cease to be a Kid-Thinker. Instead you become a Stuck-Thinker. There are two kinds of Stuck-Thinkers: Blocked-Heads and Idea Bunnies. A Blocked-Head is someone who's so convinced by what Marv says that he doesn't even know what he dreams of doing. Idea Bunnies have another problem altogether: They have so many ideas that they neglect to act on any of them.

To make your dream a reality you need both goals and actions that are specific, present, and true. It works like this:

1. Break your goal into specific, doable parts.
2. Take action on those parts immediately.
3. Ascertain that the goal you've chosen is truly something you desire—not something you're doing to please someone else.

After taking the small, specific steps toward making your dream a reality, you enter a state called the Milky Way Moment, the joyful experience of finally going from the anxiety-filled mulling to the joyous doing. Getting down to the business of making dreams happen is its own reward. With a little luck, as you're hyper-engaged in the details of making your dreams real, you may pass from the Milky Way Moment to the HourGlass—a blissful state of creative thinking in which hours go by like minutes. But if you're stuck listening to Marv, without taking any other action except to listen to him and his pessimism, he "compensates" you with the dried blade of grass—his dull, dry, tasteless, nutritionless consolation prize for your obeisance to his negativity.

Next, use your Milky Way GPS to recalibrate the trajectory of your dreams when they invariably go off course. Your Milky Way GPS consists of the following:

1. Enlisting a posse of supporters to guide you
2. Doing regular technological fasts to free your mind
3. Avoiding External Deflators, who will always tell you why you won't succeed
4. Doing the Write Your Song BBO, which is a way to take your dream and make it manifest in song form. While not actually taking shape in the real sense, your dream will have become far clearer now that you've placed it within a rhythmic and rhyming structure.

Doing the Brain Bottle Openers in this book will help you create and sustain goals that are specific, present, and true. By following this step-by-step practical guide you will learn to silence Marv, let out your Big Muse, and truly begin the process of seeing your dreams materialize.

Now think back once more to that white chalk on that black wall that I mentioned in the introduction to this book. Think about the dream that first arose in your mind when I asked you what you wanted to accomplish with your life before you die. See if you feel different now that you've been equipped with these tools and this new understanding.

Before I go, I want to leave you with this quote from the Scottish writer and mountaineer William H. Murray: "Whatever you can do, or dream you can do, begin it. Boldness has genius, power, and magic in it. Begin it now."

We all have the capacity to feel a measure of that genius, power, and magic. They are ours when we take action. The degree to which we commit ourselves to our dreams for our own betterment, and for the betterment of the world, is the degree to which William H. Murray's words will ring true. As he says, "Begin it now."

SPECIAL THANKS

FIRST AND FOREMOST to my wife, Maria, my soulmate in the purest sense of the word, and to my children: Isaac, Raina, Chaya, and Josiah (K"H). You are the wellspring of my greatest joy and the manifestation of my deepest dreams for good.

To my beloved people: Beverly and Dick Fink, Paul Himmelman and Judy Smertenko, Nina and Russell Rothman, and Arthur "Uncle Sonny" Himmelman, for always being there. And to the spirit of my late sister, Susan Shapiro-Himmelman, who is never far from my heart.

For their incredible guidance and editorial help: Lou Carlozo, Cameron Dougan, Randy Victor, and Kiki Koreshet.

For their faith, inspiration, and wonderful ideas: Jim Cohen, Holly Raider, Rob Wolcott, Rob Webb, Marty Miller, Michael Perman, Dan Leavitt, Simon Jacobson, Bob Noredeman, Jeff Victor, Jim Hershleder, David Hollander, Jessica and Josh Malkin, Brad Keywell, Laurie Sandell, Philip Nelson, Ruth and Doron Blatt, Lance Gould, Avi and Anat Shemesh, Ben Parr, Peggy Orenstein, Lynn Goldsmith, Will Powers, Kim Aiko Macpherson,

SPECIAL THANKS

Jane Wueliner, Emily Caragher, Rich Cooper, Richard Abramowitz, Steve Simons and Doni Silver Simons, David Himmelman, Jessie and David Confeld, Ray Himmelman, Michelle, Tali, Leah, and Peter Shapiro, Paul and Allison Strachman, Dana and Michael Weiss, Michael Rothman, Bob Roback, Brian Phelan, Seth Kaplan, Andy Kamman, Eric Moen, Tom Yorton, Adam Payne, Donneta Colbach, Chuck Silber, Jack Grapes, Michael Peck, Danny Siegal, David Morgan, Mitch Okmin, Kristin Mooney, Al Wolovitch, Josh Rabinowitz, Steven Shapiro, Ari Emanuel, Kirby Kim, Mark Achler, Sherman Alexie, Josh Altman, Sheldon Gomberg, Steve and Allesandra Haines, Melissa Barany, Andrea Driessen, Dan Grant, Andy Lurie, Jennifer Rudolf Walsh, Michael Kornet, Bonnie Rohm, Frank Jenks, Jeff Drooger, Debbie Gold, Jarrod Tobel, Ernie Katz, Maureen Butler, Ellen Berman, Justin Glockler, Wendi Khabie, Sam Richter, Steven Esses, Daniel Siegal, Bob Duskis, Linda Belkin, Mark Koenig, Fred Harburg, Melissa Thornley, Meira Goodfriend, Peter and Julie Weil, David Morgan, Hugh Musik, Doug Rausch, Lori Dekalo, Scott Eirinberg, Rob Schwartz, Steven Serio, Todd Stevens, Adam Grant, Tim Townsend, Alan Weinkrantz, and my friend the late Jim Schmidt, whose influence and inspiration I carry with me daily.

My gratitude to Jeanette Shaw at Penguin Random House/TarcherPerigee for her faith in me, and for using the "magic wand" of her superb editorial skills to make this book more readable and more effective than I could ever have dreamed possible.

Last but not least, thank you to Erin Malone at WME. Her guidance and encouragement have been invaluable in making this book a reality.

ABOUT THE AUTHOR

PETER HIMMELMAN is a Grammy- and Emmy-nominated musician, visual artist, and author. His company, Big Muse, unlocks the creativity of companies, organizations, and individuals, worldwide. He holds an advanced management certificate from the Kellogg School of Management at Northwestern University. Peter lives with his wife, Maria, and his African leopard tortoise, King Ferdinand, near the ocean in Santa Monica, California. When he's not on tour or giving his Big Muse seminars, he spends his days playing instruments, writing, and fielding phone calls from his four grown children, all of whom, thankfully, still need their father's advice.

For more information visit www.bigmuse.com and www.peter himmelman.com.